BYGONE BENTHAM

by

Joseph Carr

Introduced by

Peter A. Marshall

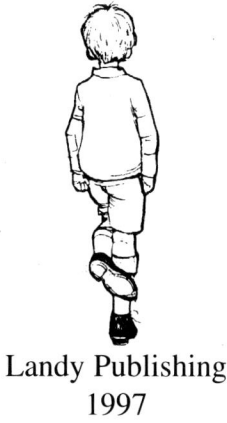

Landy Publishing
1997

© Copyright is claimed by Peter A. Marshall and Landy Publishing

British Library Cataloguing in Publication Data.
A Catalogue record for this book is available from the British Library.
ISBN 1-872895-33-6

Landy Publishing have also published:

A Blackburn Miscellany, edited by Bob Dobson
An Accrington Miscellany, edited by Bob Dobson
Accrington Observed, by Brian Brindle and Bob Dobson
In Fine Fettle, dialect verse by Peter Thornley and Michael May
Blackburns West End, by Matthew Cole
A Lancashire Look, by Benita Moore
Accrington's Changing Face, by Frank Watson and Bob Dobson
Policing Wigan, by Jim Fairhurst
A History of Pilling, by F. J. Sobee
Threads of Lancashire Life, by Winnie Bridges

A full catalogue of their publications may be had from
Landy Publishing,
3 Staining Rise, Staining, Blackpool, FY3 0BU
Tel/fax: 01253 895678

Printed by Pica Print of Low Bentham

CONTENTS.

Introduction..5

The Family of Joseph Carr. 7

Bentham - Its Past and Present 11

Reminiscences of My Native Village from 1817 to 1893 29

Personal Recollections of Lower Bentham from 1822, ...81

Obituaries of Joseph.Carr 135

List of Subscribers..138

Index of Surnames..141

The Water Fountain on Main Street, Ingleton carries the inscription:
"Memorial erected MDCCCC in memory of Joseph Carr."
Drawn by Carol J. Bentley

INTRODUCTION

Some time ago, my attention was drawn to a series of 26 articles about Bentham village and villagers which had appeared in the Lancaster Guardian between 1871 and 1897. They had been written by Joseph Carr who had associations with Bentham and Ingleton and who was as fine a local historian as any place ever had. Photocopies of the articles were obtained, and these have been transcribed to become the contents of this book. Nothing has been left out or changed, even though occasionally Carr repeated some items about which he had written earlier, but the details generally vary. The date on which an article appeared in the Lancaster Guardian is shown under each heading.

He recorded all life - the gentry, the events, the roads, the tradesmen, the wages, the costs, the drinking customs, the social conditions, the Temperance Movement, the suicides, the new buildings, the churches and the chapels. Nothing much escaped his notice and his pen. To the 26 pieces have been added, in tribute to a man to whom we owe such a lot, the two lengthy obituary notices which appeared in the Lancaster Guardian on his death in 1899. They appear to have been written by the editor - an act of praise in itself.

The members of Carrs family, who are in fact never specifically mentioned as being his relatives in these articles, have been researched. What has been discovered is presented here to help Benthamers to learn something of the man whose links with our village and with Ingleton will be valued more and more as the years pass.

Joseph Carr was a deeply religious member and preacher of the Free Church, and a strong teetotaller all his life. He was variously a schoolmaster, a missionary, a writer and a worker for social reform. He it was who first introduced tourists to Ingleton, showing them, and indeed local people as well, the beauties of the district. He wrote in the Lancaster Guardian for over half a century and the articles reprinted here cover his reminiscences of his early life in Bentham together with a contemporary account of the development of Bentham during the 20th century.

The assistance of Mrs. Muriel Humphries of Burton-in-Lonsdale, John Wilson of Tatham, Alan Duckworth of Lancaster Library, historian John Bentley of Burnley (author of Carrs Recollections of Ingleton) and his artist wife Carol, and of Ann Rothwell editor of the Lancaster Guardian, is gratefully recorded, together with appreciation for permission to include photographs from the David Johnson Collection and those provided by other local residents.

Peter Ayrton Marshall,
Low Bentham, 1997.

Main Street, High Bentham (circa 1900) at the junction with Robin Lane, looking towards the Black Bull. The publican at the Royal Oak waits to see if the solitary lady is heading his way!

THE FAMILY OF JOSEPH CARR.

Joseph Carr was descended from a long-established Ingleton family. His grandfather, also Joseph, who was born in 1739, married Isabel Armistead in 1762 at Ingleton. Their son Richard was born in Ingleton in 1778, but he moved to Bentham for work as a flax dresser and when he married in Bentham in 1811, he signed the register with his mark "X", but his wife, Dorothy, was able to write her own name. Dorothy was the daughter of Isaac Melling, a shoemaker from Wray-in-Melling, and it is interesting to note that when she was baptised in Low Bentham Church on 22nd June 1777, her mother, Mary (daughter of John and Grace Hodgson) was also baptised on the same day, being described as "an Adult Quaker".

Joseph Carr himself was baptised at Low Bentham Church on 31st January, 1813, and was brought up in the family home on Main Street, High Bentham. He was the eldest of five children, Joseph, Mary, Bella, Isaac and Ann, whose Christian names incidentally included those of all four of their grandparents. Two of his sisters, Bella and Ann, married and presumably died young as their daughters (Mary Ann, born 1836, and Margaret, born 1844) were in 1851 being looked after by Josephs parents, whilst the young girls fathers, James Sibbald (Shoemaker) and Joseph Bolton (Mechanic) worked elsewhere. Joseph Carrs mother died in 1848, but his father lived until 1861, having spent his last few years in Morecambe, before being brought back to Bentham to be buried beside his wife. Joseph himself nearly died from smallpox when he was 19 and was dangerously ill again at the age of 23, in the year in which he signed the pledge to become a total abstainer from all intoxicating drinks.

On 18th October 1843 Joseph (then described as a Schoolmaster) was married in Bentham Parish Church to Alice Balderston of Ingleton, and their daughter, Elizabeth Ann, was born in the following year. Alice was daughter of Richard Balderston of Ingleton, and her brother, Robert, lived with the Carrs at Hollin Tree, in Ingleton, for much of his life. Alice died in 1871 and was buried in Ingleton Churchyard, but her husband, lived until 1899, when he was interred in Ingleton cemetery. Their daughter was buried beside him in 1920 and it is interesting to note that on their headstone Josephs date of birth is given as 2nd December 1813, but, in 1897 he wrote that he was born on the 3rd December 1813. However, as already noted, he was baptised in January 1813 (16 months before his eldest sister), so he must actually have been born in 1812 ! Joseph Carr was generous to Ingleton village and to those around him and he managed his financial affairs so efficiently that on his death his effects were valued for probate at a mere £89 ! The obituaries which follow the main text give us a comprehensive summary of his lifes achievements.

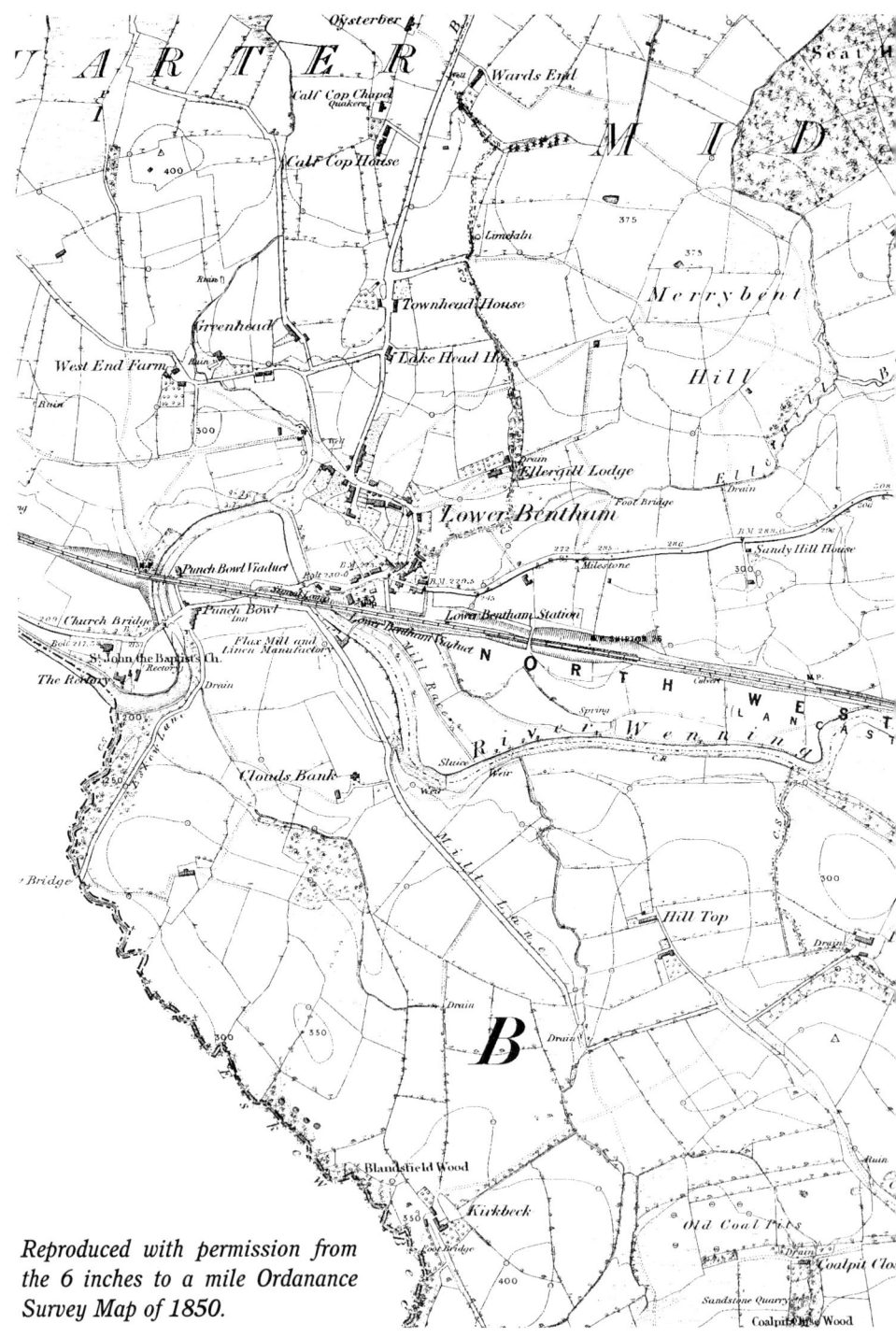

Reproduced with permission from the 6 inches to a mile Ordanance Survey Map of 1850.

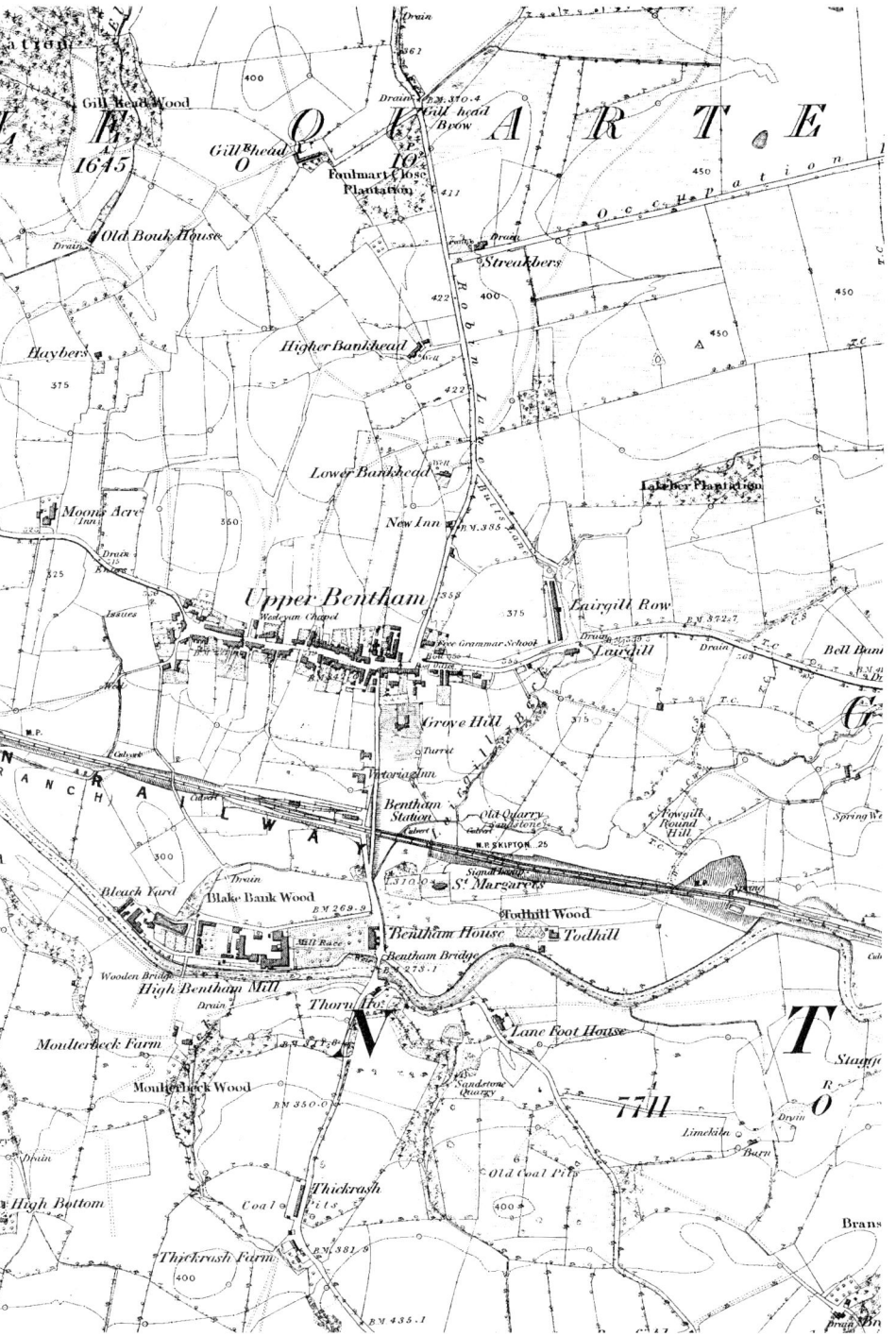

Main Street, High Bentham viewed from the top of Station Road, with cobbled pavements leading to the Post Office. (circa 1905)

BENTHAM - ITS PAST AND PRESENT

No.1 (11th November, 1871)

When a man for more than half a century has lived and moved in the ever changing circle of life, he cannot but feel an interest in comparing the past with the present. In glancing back on the thriving village of Bentham, one can have no sympathy with those men who deplore in plaintive tones the inferiority of the present age, and cry out, "*Oh, for the good old times!*" Admitting that Bentham, like neighbouring villages, is far from having arrived at the summit of human excellency, still, from whatever standpoint one may view the place and people, great changes for the better have taken place in the present century. Very creditable improvements within the time mentioned have taken place in the village, the streets, the shops, and the position and morals of the people. The village and its inhabitants of today are widely different to what they were within the memory of persons still living.

Many Old Families Have Gone

In reviewing the past, one cannot but feel regret that many of the old family names have entirely disappeared, and many families have left no descendants in the village to perpetuate their names, professions, and occupations. The Parkers, the Roughsedges, the Johnsons, the Swainsons, the Tunstalls, the Overends, the Ellershaws, the Tennants, the Guys, the Kendals, the Burtons, the Battersbys, the Heatons, the Mellings, the Wildmans, &c., &c., were once old and familiar names, but now most of them are only remembered by a few amongst the living. One cannot wander back in memory to those old Bentham families, and by recollection bring back their personal appearance, doings, and sayings, without mingled feelings of pain and pleasure. What changes in half a century take place in families as well as things, for most of the persons known in merry childhood have past from the roll of the living, and with few exceptions those who survive have long since gone from their native village.

Could the whereabouts of all the absent ones be ascertained, it would be found that amongst the dead some repose beneath the restless waves of the sea, and some on shores of foreign lands, while the living have a name and a place in every quarter of the globe. One may say that the families and names of the present inhabitants are so far changed that an old Benthamer, who has been away from the village for some years, would not know one person in twenty. In reviewing the past, one cannot but note some of the things which have fallen into merited oblivion.

The Parish Clerk

A few of the inhabitants will remember when the parish clerk, at the close of the Sabbath morning service, hurried out of the church and mounted a tombstone, when the retired worshippers gathered round him while he called the sales and other public matters which were about to take place in the neighbourhood. It was no unusual thing for the clerk, at the time of the year, to announce to men and youths the severe legal penalties which would be inflicted on them if they should, after being warned, enter the lands and woods of yeomen and farmers in the pursuit of nuts. Though there might be some excuse for our forefathers connecting such announcements with their devotions, still there need be no regret that such a custom has fallen into disuse.

Another custom in connection with the Parish Church - singing through the streets at burials - was anything but a credit to the solemnity of the occasion. "*Thee we adore*", or some other funeral dirge, used to be given out, one or two lines at once, in a drawling tone, by the parish clerk, which was sung to a dolorous tune in strains anything but melodious. The custom was long in dying out, and the principal cause of its decadence was that the thing became ridiculous when the clerk had both to line out the hymn and sing it himself. No doubt the disuse of this custom is a relief to those who have to follow their dead to the last resting place. Had the singing, on an average, been good, and persons present who had a voice for song joined in, the custom might have lingered on a few more years, but the idea of a funeral cortege pacing slowly through the streets, preceded by the parish clerk, drawling out a few words descriptive of the uncertainty of life, and then singing in no pleasant strains, without anyone to accompany him, was anything but in harmony with the sorrowful procession.

Another custom which showed the rudeness of the age in which it was practised, that of lifting on Easter Monday, has long since passed away. This was a practice which filled modest women with terror, and consequently few of them dared to leave their houses on that day. It is true that there were women of strange notions of female modesty, who rather enjoyed being tossed up in the air by a few brawny men. It was natural that women were more liable to be lifted than men. There were bold women in that day, who enjoyed lifting the men as much as the men did lifting the women. Even women were known to pull a gentleman off his horse when he was riding through Bentham, and would not permit him to continue his journey until they had tossed him up three times in the air. On some occasions men of a ruder sort would toss their victims up for a few times and then let them fall on the ground, but this cruel practice was not generally tolerated.

Chairing the Mayor

Another foolish custom which has disappeared with the past generation was that of chairing mayor on the evening following the latter fair day in June. It was a practice to select a man for the mayoralty whose brain was pretty well muddled with drink. When a man had been selected his face was blackened and his garments supplemented with things of such a metamorphosing character that his appearance caused roars of laughter. After the mayor had mounted an old chair provided for the occasion it was usual to carry him shoulder high through the street. In their route, they chiefly visited the publicans and shopkeepers.

If the mayor chanced to be a man of some wit and of very fluent tongue he sometimes made hard hits at the tradespeople, which excited much laughter and applause. If the mayor happened to be a man of few ideas and at a loss to express them in words the crowd laughed at his confusion, and were delighted to see him stuck fast in his speech. The subject of the mayor's remarks when addressing the licensed victuallers was on the dishonesty of adulterating malt liquor, diluting spirituous liquors with water and selling them for genuine articles.

If the mayor understood his duties well he would remind them of the wrong of using a piece of chalk with a nick in it when they strapped (trusted) their customers, and of selling short measure. The shopkeepers were ordered to sell good articles at a cheap rate, and to let their customers have good weight and measure. If he happened to tell them that they were not to put sand in their sugar nor wet their tobacco it was sure to cause roars of laughter. The publicans and shopkeepers were threatened with terrible pains and penalties if during the year of the mayors office they should dare to disregard his injunctions.

If the mayor and his bearers were muddled when they began the annual procession, they were so well supplied with drink on their route that generally before they had passed through the village the civic officer and his seat came tumbling down in the street, when the fun of chairing mayor passed away with the evening twilight. One of the last men that was honoured with the office of mayor was old Robert Stackhouse. Without showing any desire to diminish the amusements of the people one cannot but rejoice that a more enlightened community has allowed such barbarous customs to sink into oblivion.

HIGH BENTHAM.
William Phillipson and Son
WATCH AND CLOCK MAKERS; GOLD and SILVER WATCHES; CLOCKS, English, French, Anglo, and American; Gold ALBERTS, GUARDS; CHAINS, BROOCHES, LOCKETS, EARRINGS, STUDS, &c. Austrian Regulators, &c. Standard Gold Wedding Rings.
A WATCH CLUB held; entries can be made at any time.

No.2 (2nd December, 1871)

Horses and Carriers

In glancing over the past, one cannot but take note of the great changes which have taken place in the occupations of the people of Bentham. At one time the carrying trade was exceedingly brisk, and the tramp of horses and the rumbling of wagon wheels was a matter of some excitement in the village. Sedgwick and Son were extensive carriers of groceries and other goods between Lancaster and Bentham, and Settle and Bentham. A few of the inhabitants will remember how they were accustomed to turn their hard worked horses loose in the street without halter or attendant to find their way to the water-trough in the centre of the village called Tweed. These horses, when they happened to be in a playful mood, often caused much fear and consternation to the passers by. Old Tommy Camm used to be employed in the carriage of coal from Ingleton Colliery to the Bentham bleachworks, and old John Phipps in carting coals to Bentham Mill. Old Roger Carr, of Lowther Hill, and his sons, with their wagons and horses, generally went three times a week with goods to Lancaster and for flax for Bentham Mill. These carriers have long since passed away, and their occupations, like themselves, are now things of the past. John Varley, of Tatham, and John Lambert, of Holmes, carried on a brisk trade in meal and flour, and their numerous carts well laden with the staff of life often excited the notice of the inhabitants when they passed up the village from Lancaster. Those active and extensive dealers in bread stuffs no longer walk our streets, and their business has passed into other hands. The opening of the Little North Western Railway made a wonderful change in the carriage of goods, and in breaking up old established concerns.

For a week or more at the close of Lancaster March Assizes there used to be much excitement at Bentham. The whole village at times was moved when chaise and carriages with their liveried postilions came with judges, counsellors, lawyers, and others who were on their way to York Assizes. The King's Arms front in those days used to be crowded with gay carriages from Pritt's, King's Arms, Lancaster. The people - young and old - were wont to gather round the carriages to peep at their occupants. The staring in at the windows often attracted the attention of the judges and counsellors and caused them to question the people about things of trifling importance. A few may remember old Dennis, the village tailor, offending one of the judges by his impertinent replies.

The gay liveries of Mr. Pritt's boy postilions excited the envy of many of the village lads, who imagined the finest thing in life was driving a coach and horses. Old William Bickerstaff who was well known in Bentham half a century ago, for some years carried the mail bags, passengers, and sundry parcels between Lancaster and Bentham, but his occupation, like his life, has gone with a past generation. The coach from Lancaster to Leeds used on its going and returning to cause some stir in the village and attract idlers to the place where it stopped to take up passengers and goods, that they might see fresh faces and hear of passing events. The excitement for a time was increased when an opposition coach was brought into competition with the ordinary coach and the drivers and guards vied with each other to secure the most patronage and to pass the most quickly over their daily route. John King, a kind-hearted and unassuming gentleman of hunting notoriety, if report was correct, was far from being a gainer by his connection with this ruinous opposition. Though these notes of past scenes, persons, and pursuits are but brief, still they cannot but revive in the recollection of those who were familiar with Bentham life 50 years ago things that had long since slipped from their memories.

Hatters and Cobblers

Other trades besides that of carriers of goods and passengers have either disappeared from Bentham or been greatly diminished through other causes than that of the transit of goods by rail. The hat-making trade, which was carried on by Tennant, and afterwards by Skirrow, has entirely disappeared. At one time most of the felt and stuff hats worn by the inhabitants were made either at Bentham or Wray. Indeed, fifty years ago there were few stuff hats worn by any but the well-to-do inhabitants and workmen, and the village lads were glad to get the heavy felt hats which were made in that day. A few of the natives will still remember how their fathers used to take them to the village hatter at Easter or June fair in the morning to be fitted with new hats. It will be fresh in their memories how the hats used to be placed in rows on shelves in a large piece of furniture like a clothes press, and how hat after hat was pressed on or over the forehead of the rising youth until a proper fit had been secured. When the Bentham shopkeepers began to add to their stock in trade London and Paris fashionable hats, the local manufacture began to decline, so that now the business is defunct, and it is probable that the whiz-whiz of the hatter's bow will be heard no more.

Shoemaking at one time was a trade of some importance for the foreign as well as the home market, but now this trade has dwindled down to a very narrow compass. The principal cause of the decline in the shoemaking trade is that the leading shopkeepers deal in ready-made boots and shoes. Cheap and inferior shoes which may be obtained almost at any shop, at public auctions, and off hawkers, have all but ruined the local shoemaking trade, so that the number of village shoemakers is small, and few if any of them employ journeymen or apprentices. The Mellings, the Leaks, and the Faradays, who in their day employed many journeymen and raised a numerous race of young cordwainers, were only known to a few of the present inhabitants, and their shops have been turned into cottages.

Few persons will remember the brisk trade that was carried on at the spring and midsummer fairs, when the villagers and surrounding inhabitants were accustomed to buy their broad and narrow cloths, their woollen cord and ribbed and plain fustian. At Easter fair the clothiers used to be so numerous that their stalls used to be spread out for a considerable distance on each side of the street. The trade in drapery goods was wont to be so brisk that the high end of the village was crowded with clothier's stalls and their customers on Easter Monday. The draper's shops at Bentham are now so numerous and their stock of different kinds of cloth so extensive, that now only one or two clothiers visit the fairs. Many a spoilt child in those days was coaxed into obedience by a too indulgent mother telling him that if he would be a fine lad he should have new breeches at the fair. These old times are gone, and now instead of the people buying cloth at the fair, the custom is to get new clothes made to put on at the fair, so that now the tailor's busiest time is before the fair instead of after.

Weavers and Bentham Mill

Bentham Mill, which was originally a corn mill in the occupation of one Vipond, had experienced great changes in some of its trade departments since it was first converted into a flax mill. Though hackling by hand and machinery, spinning flax and tow, and bleaching yarns still continue, yet sailcloth, linen, and sackcloth weaving has quite disappeared. Looms at one time were common amongst the farmers in Mewith, who added that of weaving to their agricultural pursuits. These weaving farmers used to come at stated periods with their pieces in their carts to the warehouse, where they received the price of their labour, and then with merry speech and joyous hearts they returned with their wages and their warp and weft. It was a lucky thing that these fellside farmers on their way home had not like the village weavers to pass a public house, otherwise many of them might have found more than a tithe of their wages gone ere they reached their homes. Many of the village weavers were wont to drink deep after pay day.

Sailcloth weaving was extensively carried out at this time, and the rattle of shuttle was heard from early morn to late at night. The first storey of that large block of houses at the west end of the village called Scotland Row, but better known as Bedlam, was one immense weaving shed, with a double row of sailcloth looms running the whole length. This shop long ago was converted into human dwellings. The west side of the square at the east end of the village was at one time filled with looms, but now such changes have taken place in the textile craft that the shop has been made into cottage dwellings. The long row of houses on the east side of the village, called Lairgill or Kirkham, was cellared for weaving shops. For years sailcloth weaving in these cellar-shops was exceedingly brisk, and a large number of hands who lived in the upper storeys were constantly employed. Some of the old looms may still occupy their places in these cellars, but the din of shuttles, treadles, looms, and the workmen's merry sounds, have long since passed away. The ground floor of the large block of buildings between the mill and the bleach-house used to be filled with looms for the weaving of fancy and plain linen cloth. This shed, which used to be a constant scene of bustle, noise, and activity like the other weaving sheds, has experienced the fickleness of the weaving trade and become the dwellings of men employed in other departments of factory operation. Many other small places in different parts of the village which were once used as weaving shops have been converted into workmen's dwellings.

Sack making used to be carried on to a great extent, when it was no uncommon thing to see poor women who were wishful to help their husbands to maintain their large families bending beneath their load of sacking or sacks while returning or going to the mill warehouses. For the relief of married women, who have enough to do without sack making to manage their households well, it is pleasant to report that that occupation no longer exists in the village.

LOW BENTHAM READING-ROOM.

A TEA AND ENTERTAINMENT
Will be given in aid of the Low Bentham Reading-room, on Saturday, April 27th, on the occssion of the
RE-OPENING OF THE PARISH CHURCH, BENTHAM,
IN the Warehouse adjoining the Low Mills. Admission to Tea and Entertainment 1s. each. Children under Twelve years of age 8d. each. Admission to Entertainment only 3d. each. Tea at 4-30 ; Entertainment, 6-30.
Tickets may be had from any member of the Reading-room. [81]

No.3 (16*th* December, 1871)

In the second article on the past and present of Bentham there was a slight omission of the names of persons long engaged in the carrying trade. Brian Holmes, of Lairgill, was carrier for Bentham Mill. Early in the present century Holmes removed to Branstone Beck, when Charnley, who succeeded him, continued for many years to carry for Bentham Mill, first at Lairgill and afterwards at Wennington. The last-named carrier was followed by old Roger Carr, of Lowther Hill, and his sons. In describing the trades which had passed away mention should have been made of nail-making, which forty years ago was carried on by Thomas Blackburn and others.

Street Improvements

In noticing the many improvements which have taken place in Bentham one cannot but admire the changes which have taken place in the streets, the shops, and the dwellings of the inhabitants. Horse middens, cow middens, pig middens, ash middens, cesspools, and sinks were wont to occupy prominent positions in the streets, and the inhabitants were so familiar with the sight and effluvium of these breeders of stench and disease that they were seldom noticed. Slopstones and house drains were rarities, and it was common for the good housewives to throw their refuse water into the street channels to find its way from the village by three main open gutters, one on the east side of the Royal Oak, another by Tennant well on the south side of the Tweed, and the other by Duck-street. The middens and sinks have been removed, the open channels have been succeeded by covered drains, and now Bentham as far as the eye can see is a model village for cleanliness and sanitary improvements. No doubt the Bentham Sewage Authority deserve much credit for this street purgation. At a time when it was far more common than at present for working men to keep pigs, pig cotes occupied no mean place in the streets. These unseemly buildings have been entirely removed out of sight.

Old barns, shippons, and stables in the street 40 or 50 years ago were far more common than they are now. From the number of these buildings one might think that the ancient inhabitants were principally farmers. At the entrance to the village from the west there are now four old barns. A little higher up there used to be two old barns beside stable, pig cote, and shippon. One barn and the other buildings adjoining have been made into cottages. A house, grocers shop, and store-room have been made out of a portion of the other. At less than a stone throw from this place there were two barns opposite each other. A portion of one has been made into a cottage and a shop. This shop was first used as a butcher's shop, but subsequently has been used for other purposes. Not far from here there is another barn and shippon, on the south side of the street, which remain in their primitive condition. Less than 100 yards from this barn there are the remains of the old workhouse. Fifty years ago this was an old thatched building consisting of various dwellings, which were occupied by poor parishioners rent free. There are persons now living who occupied some of the dwellings at that day. For more than 30 years the old workhouse has been a ruin, and its stones piled on a heap on the west side of the new workhouse. This pile of old stones is anything but creditable to the parish authorities, and far from being ornamental to the village. Many schemes at intervals have been concocted to remedy this state of things, but hitherto they have proved abortive. Since the passing of the new Education Act various parish meetings have been held for the purpose of adopting a scheme for building a village school on the site of the old workhouse. It is to be hoped that before long the pushing men of Bentham will turn the stones and site to some public advantage. Near this place there were three old barns. The one opposite the old workhouse was turned into a blacksmiths shop by old Bob Middlebrook. The old blacksmith had a wonderful tact for relating sensational and exciting tales. On winter nights the smithy hearth used to be crowded with big lads and young men who were attracted and charmed with his smithy tales. The other barns occupy their old places and wear the same sombre appearance they did half a century ago. A few yards higher up the street there were Guy's barn and shippon. The shippon for many years was used as a joiner's shop, afterwards a tinner's shop, and now a paper hanger's sign is above the door. Near the east end of the entrance to the square, until recently stood an old thatched barn with its cracked gable end to the main street. For many years this old dilapidated barn, which was used by old John Bailey and others as a joiner's shop, was not only dangerous to the public, but it was a disgrace to the village. The old house on the opposite side of the street, which was long occupied by old James Thornton, appears to have been an old barn, as an archway was observable when it was taken down to become the site for two neat cottages. If the owners of the old barns, which still remain in the street could convert them into neat and comfortable cottages, it would not only pay, as rents in Bentham have increased much in late years, but would add greatly to the respectable appearance of the village.

New Shops

One of the greatest improvements in Bentham within the last fifty years is in the increase and commodiousness of its shops and dwellings. At the date mentioned there were very few shops which were not to be compared to the present shops for convenience and appearance. Kendal's, Burton's, Holmes', Leak's, and Miss Willan's shops, with a bakehouse and tippling shop kept by old Nancy Swinbank, would be about the number that existed at the time mentioned. Some of these shops which are now kept by Holmes, Mrs. Jackson, Bowker, and Jackson, are much improved, and some of them enlarged. There were two shops at the time near the mill, one on the north side of Wennington bridge, kept by Toulmin and then Holmes, and the other on the south side, kept by Geldard. When Mrs. Geldard began shop keeping about seventy years ago, an armchair held her merchandise. Charles Parker told her that a shop of such small dimensions would never do, and consequently she was to have a new wing built on the east side of her house for trading purposes. This shop, which still exists, and is carried on by the same family, was long patronised by the farmer weavers out of Mewith on their return from the mill with their work and wages. At this time there was a large shop kept by John Parker, of Fourstones. Though this shop was a mile and a half from Bentham an extensive business was carried on with the villagers.

The following statistical statement will show what an increase of shop accommodation, &c., has taken place within the present century, and consequently the great increase in the local trade. There are eleven grocer's shops, four draper's shops, two tinner's shops, one leather cutting shop, one ironmonger and saddler's shop, six shops for sweets, and three butcher's shops. There are also five public houses, one beer house, two spirit merchants, one maltster, and three dealers in bone and other manures. One might add to the number shoemakers, dressmakers, cloggers, &c., but none of them keep shops for the exhibition and sale of their handicraft. In specifying the shops either made out of old barns or newly constructed, one may begin with the grocers shop on the west side of the Methodist Chapel. This shop, which was made out of an old barn, had for many years a thriving home and county trade under the stirring management of Henry Carr. A few years ago the same successful tradesman bought the land and house on the east side of the Methodist Chapel, and build a substantial and commodious grocers shop on what used to be known as Sedgwick Front. Robert Ward, who was a plodding and successful packman at the beginning of the present century, bought Middlebrook's old smithy and the adjoining house, out of which he made a first-rate drapers shop and house. The premises are so far improved outwardly as well as inwardly that they have quite a neat appearance. This shop which took the lead from the first in the drapery business has not maintained its position, but has so far over-grown itself that a large branch and successful business has been established at Ingleton. Thomas Greenep's house and shop, which were old buildings in his school-boy days, have undergone similar improvements to those of Robert Ward's (now Quinlan's). On the same side of the street, with only an old barn and shippon between, stands Stephenson's drapers shop, which is a very respectable building, and well adapted for business purposes. This shop and house were built by Thomas Blackburn, nail maker, (who, with his family, emigrated to America) on the site of an old thatched house, pig-cote, and pig-yard. Robert Jackson, a pushing and thriving tradesman, who has greatly enlarged the shop originally carried on by Miss Willan, carries on an extensive business in groceries and crockery. He lately purchased the row of houses known as Scotts Houses (originally Guys), which he has roofed afresh, and done other considerable repairs. Holmes', Mrs. Jackson's, Wilcock's, and the adjoining draper's shops have undergone great changes for the better within the memory of the living.

Mrs. Jackson's shop was opened by the Co-operative Society perhaps forty or fifty years ago, but it soon became defunct. A few will remember the sign above the door - *"United we stand; divided we fall."* As the Society did not stand, one may imagine that disunion hastened its decadence. The new Co-operative Society carries on an exclusive trade in groceries and other goods in the new warehouse. One of the finest grocers shops in the village, and one that would not disgrace a town of much larger dimensions, is Gornall's. This shop, which has a good frontage to the main street, stands on the site of the unseemly old barn already mentioned as a joiners shop. In addition to the shop there is a large and genteel house adjoining, facing the east with iron palisades on the front and a wall on the north surmounted with some of the finest and most fantastic stones that were ever gathered from limestone rocks. Another grocer's shop on the opposite side of the street occupied by Christopher Knowles, well merits a passing remark. This shop, the old Kings Arms, was long the head public house in the village. Amongst the many strange things which have happened at this ancient hostelry the writer well remembers when a boy being in one of the parlours, and with wondering eyes watching the late Dr. Burrow blowing with a pair of bellows into a Wray mans mouth to resuscitate a life which had been destroyed in a drunken row or fight in the Mill-lane. The proprietor of Grove Hill who a few years ago bought the Kings Arms off Atkinson, the landlord who was retiring from business, determined that for the future the old inn should be let for the sale of food instead of intoxicating drinks. C. Knowles, a man who has risen by his industry and sobriety to circumstances of comfort and respectability, recently became the purchaser of the shop and house he had occupied since the Kings Arms ceased to be a public house. Considerable alteration and improvements have just been finished, so that on one side of the entrance is a large grocer's shop, and on the other side a commodious refreshment room for tea, coffee, &c. It is rather singular that this thriving shop-keeper made the Black Horse beerhouse into a shop, then the beerhouse at the new workhouse, and now the Kings Arms.

Recent New Houses

Before concluding this article on the streets and shops of Bentham, a few words may be said on the houses which have been built within the last 50 or 60 years. The boundaries of the village on the west side have not been extended within the memory of the oldest living inhabitant. In Duck or Duke Street a row of cottages were built by John Parker, of Fourstones. Scotland Row, or Bedlam, New Kirkham or Lairgill, two rows of houses at the mill and the row at Thickrash, were built by the old mill company for their hands. Many of those houses were not planned for the comfort and convenience of the tenants but for paying a large percentage. For instance, Bedlam, where families live one above another on the old Scotch plan. There can be neither decency, health, nor comfort where a large family, with the addition at times of lodgers, have but two rooms, one to live in and the other to sleep in. Fifty or sixty years ago there was not a gentlemans house in the village excepting what was called the great house near the Brown Cow. At the time referred to there was scarcely a house with a parlour in it with the exception of public houses. Grove Hill, now the beautiful mansion of Mr. Rice, which was built by the late Mr. Johnson a little over sixty years ago, stands a little out of the village. Between forty and fifty years ago houses of larger dimensions and with more regard for comfort began to be built. Richard Hay, who kept a meal and flour shop in Mewith, built an excellent grocers shop and house on the hill behind the hospital, and on the south side of the road. During his life he carried on an extensive business in the locality. He was one of the first men who began to build cottages on an improved plan. The row of houses between his house and the hospital are neat and comfortable dwellings. John Bailey, at slightly later date, built two good houses not far from the Kings Arms, on the west side of the mill lane. Other good houses have been built near the Kings Arms. Richard Butterfield, a native of the place, and an extensive cattle dealer, has built many neat cottages in the Kings Arms old yard. Three excellent and ornamental cottages have been built on the site of an old house and barn near the Tweed, by Mr. Rice. These cottages and the neat Friends Meetinghouse add greatly to the appearance of the village. Near these houses on the opposite side of the street a row of neat cottages have been made out of two old cottages and some buildings which were once occupied by the late John Guy. The Victoria Hotel, near the Midland Railway Station, which is a good modern building, was built by the late Henry Langstreth, who in ones boyhood was the merry and good-tempered hostler at the Kings Arms. A good house and shop have just been built near the Victoria Hotel, by Francis Holmes painter and tinman. John Slinger, another Benthamer who has succeeded in business as slater and plasterer, has just built four excellent houses on the hill on the east side of the Free Grammar School. Had such houses been built sixty years ago they would have remained tenantless unless the owner would have let them at a nominal rent. Near the Tweed many cottages have been built by Jackman and his sons on ground that originally belonged to old Bob Sharp. This street, which according to report, is named Jackman street, is the fruit of their plodding and persevering industry as slaters and plasterers at Bentham.

Many old houses have been much improved inwardly and outwardly, but to mention them singly would add too much to this already lengthy article. The old public houses, the Black Bull and Brown Cow, have not undergone much improvement during the present century, and their outward appearance is little or any different to what it was 50 years ago. The Royal Oak, which was long carried on by old Deborah Battersby, was taken down and rebuilt, when it fell into the hands of the Burrows, of Guy Hill. This old public house which was much enlarged and constructed on an improved plan is now a very substantial and respectable looking village inn. Though there are too many cottages in Bentham which on account of their single bedrooms are far from being decent, healthy, or convenient for large families, still it is pleasant to see what a large number of comfortable and good looking houses for the professional and other classes have been built within the last thirty or forty years.

BENTHAM.
PAPERHANGINGS! PAPERHANGINGS!!

WILLIAM GREENEP,
PLUMBER, PAINTER, AND PAPERHANGER,
BEGS to call the attention of the Public to his New and Choice STOCK of PAPER HANGINGS for 1878, which he is prepared to offer at very reasonable prices.
Pattern Books forwarded to any address. [733

No.4 (6th January, 1872)

However great and much admired may be the improvements in a town or village in matters of trade, shops, dwellings, and streets, most persons will be ready to admit that such things are only secondary to a steady and constant advancement in the education and morals of the people. In social order, refinement of manners, honest industry, and improvement in morals, Bentham occupies no second place amongst the villages in the district. Without risking a statement that Bentham has reached anything like what it might have done in education, morals and religion, it may be affirmed that during the present century, there has been a great reformation in the manners of the people. A review of the great change which has taken place for the better, though confined to a small thriving village like Bentham, cannot but be interesting to all men who are wishful to see improvement in the human race. To make this article more interesting and striking, it may be arranged under various sections.

Drinking and Fighting

Forty or fifty years ago, drinking and fighting at fairs and on market days were of common occurrence. Two or three fights on a market day were looked upon as a matter of course. At fairs there used to be terrible rows. Parish constables had little influence to check such pugilistic encounters. Indeed parish constables generally made themselves scarce when a row began. The writer remembers putting an end to three fights within an hour at the low end of the village. As four of the public-houses were at the east end of the village, it was, as a rule, the centre of all the battles. It was common for the roughs of Ingleton to go to Bentham fair for a fight. As many of the Benthamers were of the same spirit, it was a practice to attend fairs to kick up rows. On one occasion, in the time of Charles Parker, there was a terribly bloody encounter at Clapham fair. Many of the young hecklers from Bentham mill made an onslaught on some of the Claphamers in a dancing-room, when the lights were put out, and a regular fight of fists and feet began. One of the Bentham party being an Hibernian, he wrenched a foot from one of the forms, when, in shillelagh fashion, he yielded it with terrible effect on the skulls, arms, and shoulders of the Claphamers. Many of the timid of both sides adopted many manoeuvres to escape broken heads and limbs. Little Harry Raby, one of the Bentham hecklers, concealed himself under a bed in another room, and when he was followed by others who had taken flight, his question was, "*A Benthamer or a Claphamer?*". If the latter, he kicked with all his might, if one of his own party he gave him shelter.

Men not only fought when under the maddening influence of drink, but when they were sober. Many still remember when Hewitson and Cocking fought in the croft adjoining the Kings Arms. The excitement was great, the field was crowded, and the trees at Mill Lane side were black with boys and men. Lowther and another fought a pitched battle for a sovereign a side in a field near Lairgill. Sometimes battles were attended with fearful consequences. One Huggon fought with a man of the name of

Smithers in the Mill Lane near Grove Hill, when a blow beneath the ear felled Smithers to the ground dead. On another fight near the Tweed, on a Saturday night, one of the young men, who was stabbed by his opponent, narrowly escaped with his life. At this time of the history of Bentham, the hecklers and weavers were much addicted to drinking. On the day the weavers took in their work, it was a common thing to see on their return their barrows with their warps and weft standing at the Black Bull and Royal Oak doors, whilst they called for what they considered needful refreshment. The hecklers, who were only paid once a month, used to spend large portions of their wages after receiving their pay. With some of them, a weeks spreeing was no unusual thing. To make up lost time in the last week of the month, which was called "*screw*" week, they had to do nearly double work. It was also a common practice to have drink in the shop when a kind of communism prevailed. When they drank too deeply to follow their work, if the weather was favourable, they went into the fields to continue their fuddle with new milk and rum. Footings and loosings often lead to much drinking.

The writer, though very young, never can forget the bacchanalian scenes which took place on the Black Bull front before Parson Wigglesworth's hounds returned to Slaidburn after the yearly hunt. For many years these hounds, which were under the charge of John Ayrton, came to hunt on Queen Catherine's Day. On the day following, before they started for home, it was usual for the patrons of the hunt and their friends to drown their senses in bowls of punch. The last bowl was sometimes drunk at the door. On the occasion referred to the jolly sportsmen took hold of each others hands and danced round, after the fashion of wild Indians, accompanying their movements with shouting, "*Open your mouths and gallop it in, and gallop it in!*" Drinking was not confined to hecklers and weavers, for some of the inhabitants used to be drunk daily for weeks. Old Tom Ellershaw, one of the largest landholders in the village, was in the habit of getting drunk at the Brown Cow two or three times a day. Many of the farmers who attended the market made it a rule never to leave it sober. These things have happily passed away.

Works of Mischief

Midnight scenes of a mischievous character were of common occurrence. Some nights were considered more favourable for the doing of mischief than others. Saturday night was generally selected for the purpose, after the young men had been primed with drink for the doing of reckless actions. It was no unusual thing to find on a Sunday morning, at the Cross or the Square end, washing pots, dolly tubs, signs, and a variety of other domestic articles, all mixed together in the wildest confusion. When the message was reported through the village that if anyone had lost any pots and pans they would find them at the Cross, the doers of mischief would stand by to witness the excitement and laugh at the perplexity of those who had some difficulty in picking out their lost articles. Knocking at folks doors at untimely hours of the night to disturb their sleep or their fears was a favourite amusement. The Fifth of November was generally the crowning night for mischief. Fierce and desperate young men appeared to lose all regard for their neighbours property, consequently gates, doors, wheels, and anything and everything within their reach of an inflammable character was made to contribute to the bonfire on the 5th of November.

Some few will remember when Charnley's horses and wagons had to be driven through a bonfire near Moons Acre. At the time there were a house and a malt-kiln belonging to Mr. John Titterington in an unfinished state. In consequence of the new building, a long thorn fence on the roadside had been stubbed and as the thorns and roots were handy for commemorating the gunpowder treason and plot, a fire was made in the public road. As there was much loose timber about for building purposes, John Cumberland, the joiner, of Low Bentham, came up with a gun and threatened to shoot the first that should dare to meddle with his timber. Amidst wild shouts and yells these dreadnought young men threw peasticks, thorn bushes, and other combustibles on the devouring flames, the lurid light of which and the crackling gave unbounded excitement to their passions. A sudden noise like the rumbling of wheels caused a pause in their revelry, and when it was ascertained that it was Charnley's wagon laden with goods from Bentham Mill for Lancaster that was drawing near, their first impulse was to flee and leave the highway barricaded with flying sparks, rolling smoke, and leaping flames. A better thought coming over them, some of the stalwart youths pushed the fire as much as possible to one side of the road, and when the wagoner with his team drew near, they offered to take hold of his horses heads, while he with his whip and inspiriting words should urge them through the scattered firebrands, smoke and flames. The plan succeeded, and it was the first and last time that a wagoner and his horses had to pass through such a fiery ordeal. To the credit of Bentham, such things are now unknown.

Rudeness of Some of the People

Refinement of manners was little practised except by a few of the inhabitants of those days. Without implicating all the people, we may say that there was much rudeness among men, women, and children. There were a few women who were in the habit of seeking their husbands when they had no objection to drink a glass and sing a song to please the company. It was not uncommon for those women, on their way home, to open peoples doors and to shout into their houses in a rude and disguised voice. Some of the young women, when strangers walked through the village, would walk stealthily behind them and make wry faces. If an Irishman happened to pass through the street, some of the children would be sure to shout, "Hurrah, Pat!" On a Sunday night, young men were accustomed to stand in a crowd at Tunstall's house corner, near the Cross, and make rude remarks of passers by loud enough for them to hear. This rude custom had such a deterring effect on women that few of them dared to pass these street-corner idlers on a Sunday night. It is well that these and such like acts of rudeness are things of the past.

Sabbath Desecration

Though men cannot be coerced by Acts of Parliament or otherwise to keep the Sabbath-day holy, still a decent outward observance of the Lords day is favourable to the health and good order of the community. Football, spell and knur, bandy cat, chasing birds, and trail hunt used to be the Sundays amusements in winter. A few years ago there were old men living who could remember when young men took the football with them to Low Bentham church, and as soon as the morning service was over they threw it down in the churchyard and began their Sunday play.

In chasing birds, young men and boys were each furnished with long sticks, and then one party took one side of the hedge and the other the opposite side, when they chased every bird they might espy to death. The robin redbreast generally afforded them the most sport, as when they were hotly pursued they would not fly from hedge to hedge. Married and young men who played at spell and knur generally did so for money. In a trail hunt, a piece of carrion was generally tied to a length of rope, when someone swift of foot ran over hedge, and field, and dyke, and when he had been allowed to have a good start a number of dogs was set on his trail. In summer the young men used to play nearly all the Sunday afternoon at hand ball, either at Kings Arms house-end, the old poorhouse gable-end, or against a barn near the Methodist Chapel, or at marbles in the street. Lads were in the habit of flying kites in the street, playing at marbles and spinning tops, throwing the ball, and ball in the cap. Sometimes scores of boys and girls ran the whole length of the village playing at *"Thread my needle, set, set, set."* The weavers at the little colony called New Kirkham spent their Sundays in summer chiefly playing at nine-pins. Many of them who stripped to this exercise were unwashed and unshaven. As a rule, the men who spent their Sabbaths in this way were slovenly in their dress and rude in their manners. All this Sabbath desecration has passed away, and the Lords day is observed with far more decency than formerly.

Plainess of Speech and Dress

Were people now to speak as they did forty or fifty years ago, they would be considered very rude. It was usual when people were asked a question which they did not distinctly hear, to say with a drawl, *"What?"* or, *"What do you say?"* Such expressions as *"Sir"*, *"Ma'am"*, or, *"I beg your pardon"*, were not common words in the village vocabulary. Many well remember that forty or fifty years ago there was not a single person in the village who was spoken of as Mr., Mrs., or Miss. One did hear some persons say Mr. Johnson, of Grove Hill, and Mr. Roughsedge, and Mr. Overend of the mill. Mr. Roughsedge's predecessor was always spoken of as Charles Parker. The inhabitants, with rare exceptions, spoke the broad Yorkshire dialect. Had anyone attempted greater refinement of speech, it would have been pronounced knacking.

The people were as plain in their dress as their speech. Tradespeople and workmen were plainly and inexpensively dressed. Clogs and shoes, which were all home made, were made for ease and comfort rather than to make people appear to have nice feet. As people wished to get all the wear that they could out of their shoes, they were periodically soaked with train oil rather than made to shine with blacking. Top coats for men and boys were almost unknown. Pocket handkerchiefs were scarce articles indeed. The second master of the Grammar School dispensed with this article now so common, and a few of his pupils may still remember his scientific method of relieving his nasal of its secretions. Boys were wont to use their jacket cuffs.

The few Quakers of that day were models of plainness in dress. The tunnel-shaped bonnets, single-bordered caps, close-fitting dresses, and plain shawls, passed away with Mary Townson and Grace Bellman. The costume of those days never varied with the Friends. The Friends of today are much more modern in the fashion of their garments, still there appears to be nothing extravagant or gaudy in their apparel. In dress it is well to be plain and not above ones means and station, and to have a regard for our garments being made more to conduce to health and comfort than to outward show.

The Methodists were near to the Friends in plainness of dress. The women had plain bonnets, single-bordered caps, and close fitting gowns, and the men, though they had not broad brimmed hats and single coat collars, still their dress was remarkably plain. More than thirty years ago a love for dress began to show itself in the youthful members of this society. Some of the old members began to be uneasy on account of this increasing conformity to the world. The writer remembers well attending a meeting at Over Houses when good old Nathan Shackleton, in his prayer after the sermon, said, "*Lord keep pride out of Bentham Chapel.*" Old William Braithwaite, a preacher of the old school, some years ago when preaching in Bentham Chapel, seeing many of the young men and women with their hair fashionably arranged, rudely remarked, "*There has been a whirl blast from the nether regions to turn your hair wrong side up.*" Had a local preacher brushed his hair on one side, smoothed it with a little oil, and worn a dickey, he would have been set down as a fop, and unfit for the Methodist pulpit. What a contrast between the plain bonnets, unbraided hair, and flounceless gowns of the women of the past with the little bonnets decked with gay artificials, the huge prominences behind the head, and the gaudy dresses of women of modern times.

As church people did not make the same pretension to religion as the Methodists and the Friends their more fashionable dresses were not much noticed. Without accusing or excusing people on account of their dress, still it may be said that many servant girls and mill girls dress finer than quality, as they were called, dressed 40 years ago. Though there is a marked and substantial improvement in the education and speech of the people, still an excess in gaudy apparel is no improvement on the plainness of a past generation.

One cannot conclude this article without noticing one thing which cannot from any standpoint be considered an improvement on a past age, and that is the injurious and very prevalent habit of boys in their teens smoking and chewing tobacco. Half a century ago though smoking was rather common with young men and married men, still a boy in his teens durst not have gone smoking through the street by day light. It is really a shame to see lads just out of their petticoats smoking without the least concern, as if they were men. It is no mark of an advanced race to allow lads to smoke as British Workmen. Some of their cheeks are pale and thin enough, without making them more so with tobacco. What are fathers doing to allow their lads to waste their money and injure their health with tobacco?

Town End, High Bentham, looking past Parkinson's Farm towards Bentham Hall, which was built in 1908. A solitary telegraph pole is the forerunner of things to come.

High Bentham viewed from the south-west, with Wennington Mills dominating the foreground.

REMINISCENCES OF MY NATIVE VILLAGE
FROM 1817 TO 1893

No.1 (7th October, 1893)

Looking back seventy-five years appears a much shorter time than the same number of years to come. My memory faintly carries me back to 1815, when a general illumination took place to celebrate the victory of the battle of Waterloo. The glare of a multitude of lighted candles in the windows of Mr. T. H. Johnson, Grove Hill, made such a vivid impression on a mere child that the event is still remembered. It is likely that there is not a single person in the village who remembers that Waterloo illumination. It may be imagined what are the feelings of a man when he walks through the streets of his native village, and brings to his remembrance the families who lived in all the houses seventy-five years ago, and how there is not one of them living. Not a single person is living who was alive when I was five years old. The last of the inhabitants of that date was the late John Skirrow, who passed away a year or two ago, when he was between eighty and ninety years of age. It must be a marvellous instance of good health when it is remembered that all the play-mates of my boyhood and the companions of my young manhood have been many years in their graves, while I am hale and active, and as to memory and intellect not consciously different to what I was in the twenty-first year of my age. I feel I am a young man domiciled in a decaying tenement, or as St. Paul says, *"Though our outward man perish, yet the inward man is renewed day by day."* The secret of how to live a long and healthy life is not so secret if men were willing to learn it. It is not a difficult thing to show how a man of eighty years of age may be a comparatively young man.

When one thinks of the inhabitants of ones native village who departed sixty or seventy years ago many things pleasant and unpleasant come to ones mind as if they were only things of yesterday. This looking backwards makes one feel as if one were out of touch with the present generation, for there is not a solitary person who can say we did this or that thing when we were boys. If I walk through the streets I meet no one whom I knew in my boyhood. If I go to the Parish Church there is no one there who sat with me when I was a Church Sunday scholar. If I go to the Methodist Chapel, the Friends Meeting House, either at Higher or Lower Bentham, or St. Margarets Church, it is still the same. Death in seventy-five years has removed all the inhabitants within my knowledge.

Old Inhabitants

Another remarkable fact in this local history is that there are comparatively few of the descendants of the old Bentham families living in the village. In this sense the inhabitants of Bentham have all but been changed within one mans life. The following named inhabitants are descendants of old Bentham families:- Mr. W.

Greenep is on his mothers side a branch of the Leaks and Mellings. His great grandfathers were the principal shoemakers in the district, and in addition to their local trade, they did a considerable business at Clitheroe and the neighbourhood. The Mellings did part in the export trade. The Stephensons and the Sandersons are branches of old Lawrence Stephenson and Anthony Nicholson. Mr. Richard Sanderson's family's great grandmother was a daughter of Lawrence Stephenson, who carried on the business of tailoring and baking. When he began business at Bentham he went out as was the custom at that day to make clothes at the houses of his customers, at sixpence a day and his meat. The Holmes are descendants of old Brian Holmes, farmer, Lairgill. Mrs. Robert Shuttleworth is a branch on her grandmother's side of an old family of the name of Hardy. Miss Wilson and her two sisters have sprung from two old families of the names of Wilson and Overend. Their great maternal grandfather was Justice Overend a noted man in his day. Mr. J. Bellman Thornton, and his sister, Mrs. I. Melling, are of the Thornton family, once numerous in the village. Miss Willan is a solitary branch of the Swainson family. Mr. Swainson was a prominent man in the village and district in making wills and other legal documents.

Mrs. Wilcock, who lives near Bentham House, is an offshoot of the Geldards. Her uncle, the late Thomas Geldard, about the close of the last or the beginning of the present century, was the post boy for Charles Parker, the managing partner of the Bentham Mills. At that time the post office was at the Blue Hall, Ingleton, and Thomas Geldard, the post boy, travelled with and for mill letters twice a week. The Skirrows are a branch of an old Wray family, and their fore-elder, John Skirrow, for a long series of years was the principal hat maker for Bentham and the neighbourhood. He succeeded an old hat maker of the name of Tennant. At his death the business declined and shortly became one of the extinct trades of Bentham. The name of Tennant is still kept in remembrance by an old well on the south side of the buildings once occupied as the hatters shop. It was a noted spring of water before the Midland railway was made, and it was a common saying, "*If you want a cup of good tea, fetch it from Tennants well.*" The spring was mysteriously cut off during the making of the Little North Western Railway, and it has been dry ever since. The Slingers are the offspring of the Clarkes and the Slingers. The Clarkes were of an older Bentham family than the Slingers. Mr. Richard Smith comes from an old family of Smiths who lived in the square over seventy years ago.

The Phillipsons

The Phillipsons are a branch of the Phillipsons and Burrows. The great grandmother of the younger branch was the sister of Arthur Burrow, once so noted in the neighbourhood for his perpetual motion. In 1820 the Methodist Chapel was opened for religious service and a Sunday School. Old George and Margaret Phillipson, two of their daughters, and their son George, were amongst the first teachers. Mrs. Head, Temperance Hotel, and her relatives are of an old family of Wilcocks, once numerous in the village and neighbourhood. Many of the male branch were cabinet makers and bought clocks of Mr. J. Muncaster, Lancaster, and fitted them in beautiful oak and mahogany cases and sold them to young men just married or about to be married on the terms payment by instalments. The prices were from £8 to £9 each. The writer has one of these clocks and though it was made before he was born it is still in good going order. Some of the Wilcocks are descendants of old James Wilcock, cabinet maker and victualler, Punch Bowl Inn, Low Bentham. A younger branch of them was long employed at Messrs. Gillow's cabinet works, Lancaster.

In addition to the above named branches of old Bentham families there are a few descendants of old families outside the village but in its parish. The following from Mewith may be mentioned. Mr. Geo. Sedgwick, from the Sedgwicks of Staggarth, the Procters, Mill-dam, and Marshall, Burnmoor side. One of this branch, the Rev. Mr. Marshall, was for a long series of years the able and much esteemed head master of Benthams Collingwood Grammar School. Prior to his removal to Darlington for many years he did clerical service at Chapel-le-Dale. There are a few descendants of two old yeoman families on the north side of the river Wenning, the Hullys and the Battersbys. The late John Skirrow's family by the mothers side are a branch of the Hullys.

Francis Hully

This name brings to ones remembrance a rather laughable instance in sporting life. Over sixty years ago their late grandfather, Francis Hully, decided to add to his winter sports that of coursing. One day when he and his party were coursing on the north side of Lower Bentham in the rough pasture lands in the direction of Whinny Lane, they decided to conclude the days sport. Mr. Roughsedge, of Bentham House, was much opposed to Mr. Hully's coursing near his domains, as they were well stocked with game. On this occasion there occurred a favourable opportunity of showing it. The dogs and the men on their way home passed through Whinny Lane and the Seat Hall great nursery into a rough pasture in which there was another plantation of older growth. Though the foot road to Bentham passed through it, Mr. Hully and party for nearness decided to go round a circular portion of it and take the pathway on the other side. Two persons walking in opposite directions at this portion of the wood would nearly meet before sighting each other. I, a youth, was one of the party, and remember well the surprise that ensued when Mr. Roughsedge and his gamekeeper and dogs suddenly met us at the roundest portion of the wood. Mr. Roughsedges anger was aroused to a high pitch when he said to Robert Titterton, "Shoot the greyhounds." It was well for Mr. Roughsedge that his gamekeeper was of a more sober character, and no doubt he repented of his rash command as he allowed the trespass to pass without further notice.

Another of the old outside families was James Easterby, of Foulgill, near Bentham. He was a dealer in cattle, and when he used to meet his companion dealers and friends at the Royal Oak he was wont to cause roars of laughter with his amusing tales connected with money and cattle traffic. As far as my knowledge is concerned the name Battersby has disappeared from Bentham names. There is a retired grandson at Ingleton. The female branch is continued in the family of the Butterfields.

No.2 (14th October, 1893)

The Gentry and Tradespeople of Bentham, &c.

At the date of about 1820 there were comparatively few men or women locally included amongst the gentry, or what was then called quality. I cannot remember one person from the east to the west end of the village called Mr. or Mrs., except for the following persons:- Mr. Johnson, Grove Hill; Mr. Edward Heaton, who occupied the premises, a part of which is now the Horse and Farrier Inn. Married and single women were spoken of as Nanny, Jinnie, Betty, Moll or Molly, Mag or Maggie, etc. Sometimes men and women were called by their proper Christian names when no abbreviations could be found for them. The villagers with few exceptions spoke in the local dialect. Sometimes young women went into service in Manchester, London, and other large towns, and, when they, after a few years service, returned to their homes, they spoke what their friends called "*imitating fine folks,*" or "*knackin.*" When some of these young women, who preferred going to the mill to domestic service, made occasional slips of the tongue, they were accustomed to hear such remarks as "*Thou spins it gay fine, and then thou spoils it wi' spinnin' it thick.*" This was a reference to counts in yarns.

It would be misleading to insinuate that the inhabitants of Bentham were vulgar and ignorant, for they were not so. There were "*roughs*" amongst the young men, and some drunkards and poachers, same as in the neighbouring villages, but with these exceptions they were homely and kindly disposed towards each other. When a change came over the villagers on account of families more fashionable than they settling amongst them, one heard occasionally Mr., Mrs., Miss, and Sir. When I was about half advanced in my teens it was with some trepidation that I dared to speak in words as pronounced in Walkers dictionary. At the time there were not more than three or four young men who made any pretence to speak their mother tongue as it was printed. The late John Greenep, who for many years was the efficient and exemplary second master of Collingwood Grammar School and correspondent to the Lancaster Guardian was one of the four. Since that day the schoolmaster has been abroad and the inhabitants now for general correct talking will bear comparison with their neighbouring villages.

From what has been already stated it will be noticed that there were not many wealthy people in the village seventy years ago. What was wealth then would be considered a moderate income now. When I was a big lad there was a great wedding of an only daughter, which was a rare occurrence in the village and was much talked about. She was an amiable woman and of a kindly disposition. It was said she would have a good fortune, as she was heir to an estate which had cost £700. Millionaires may laugh at it, but at the time it stood high in the estimation of men who loved money.

The Land Owners

The Mill Company were the largest, as they held a number of farms in addition to their extensive cottage property. Mr. Johnson held in land the Grove Hill estate, Big Thornber, and after the death of Miss Grace Tunstall, Low Bottom. These estates were sold after Mr. Johnson's death. The Tunstall family had retired from business when I was a boy and lived in the house occupied by Miss Willan. Mr. Thomas Ellershaw, who lived in an ancient mansion near the west end of the village, was also one of the independent landowners.

There were other owners of smaller portions of land, but not sufficient to support their families. Amongst those were branches of the Melling family, the Croft's, the Skirrow's, the Lupton's, the Guy's, and the Holmes'. There might be some families who had landed property in other parishes, but if there were it would be a solitary one or two. When I was almost too young to remember much, a Quaker family of the name of Kendal left the shop now a grocer and chemist shop occupied by Mr. Holmes, and went to live on their estate, Bracking Hill, on the north side of Low Bentham.

The Old Tradesmen of 1820.

Licensed victuallers - Royal Oak, Deborah Battersby; Black Bull, Deborah Wilkinson; Brown Cow, Thomas Parkin; Kings Arms, John Cook; H. Burrow, surgeon; Edward Heaton, druggist, gardener, and bookseller; Joseph Carr, cooper; Christopher Ellershaw, plumber, tinman, &c.; Richard Clark, shuttlemaker; John Skirrow, hatter; Lawrence Stephenson, tailor, &c.; William Wildman and John Silverwood, masons; Michael Slinger, slater, plasterer, and weaver; John Leak, sen., John Melling, and John Leak, jun., shoemakers; Robert Middlebrook & Sons, blacksmiths; Mary Townson, linen draper and general dealer; Edward Wildman, likeness taker, schoolmaster, &c.; butchers, William Armistead, Richard Shepherd, Thomas Bentham, Thos. Metcalfe; dealers in flour, corn, &c., Robert Sharp, Nancy Swinbank, Robert Titterington; Christopher Titterington, clog, sole makers, &c.; Joseph Bradshaw and Geo. Swales, village and travelling dealers in pots &c.; Jas. Burton, James Moore, Thomas Holmes, and John Leak, jun., grocers; John Barker, pattern and clog maker and postmaster; straw hat maker, Isabella Clark; John Sedgwick and Son, carriers; John Bailiff and Sons, joiners and wheelwrights; Hornby and Co., flax and tow spinners, manufacturers of linen.

A Fatal Fight

Some of the above written names bring very forcibly to ones memory things grave and gay which caused much gossip in the village and neighbourhood. A very distressing fatal fight took place in the Mill lane about the beginning of November, 1823. A man of the name of Smithers, a collier from Wray, and Huggon, of Cowan Bridge, whilst drinking at the Kings Arms, quarrelled over some provoking matter to such a pitch that nothing but a fight could settle the dispute. Not many rounds had been fought before Huggon gave Smithers a fatal blow, when he was carried into a small parlour on the right hand side of the house part. Young Dr. Burrow, who had but recently commenced his medical practice at Bentham, was called in.

The utmost excitement was caused in the village, and crowds of people gathered round the inn door. Though I was a boy of ten years of age, I was allowed to enter the room and look on while Dr. Burrow was trying to inflate the mans lungs and resuscitate suspended life. After using for some time all the means available, the doctor pronounced that the man was dead. Much sorrow was felt by the crowd, as well as by the deceaseds relatives and friends.

At the inquest on the 8th of November the jury brought in a verdict of manslaughter, when the prisoner was committed to take his trial at the ensuing York assizes. After the trial was over, the excitement in the village was revived, and the people generally wanted to hear or read the verdict. Huggon in one sense as not to blame, for if it had not been for the accursed drink on his brain he would not have done the fatal deed. When a man is drunk and disorderly, which is temporary insanity, the police should have power to confine him until he comes to his senses at the expense of the landlord who last sold him drink. This appears preferable to summoning him and bringing him before the magistrates.

A Gentlemen's Argument

On one occasion a harmless but laughable affair took place between Mr. Johnson, of Grove Hill, and Mr. Roughsedge, of Bentham House. It was considered something romantic and out of place for two of the leading gentlemen of the village to have a quarrel. Mr. Johnson was an ardent lover of forest trees and he spent a large sum of money in planting them on the Grove Hill and Thornber estates. He planted them in hedge rows as well as in enclosures. Most of those trees in the Mill Lane, in the Grove Hill grounds, and in the land adjoining the vicarage, which was then part of the Grove Hill estate, were planted by him. The southern portions of these lands formed the boundary fence of the Mill Holme which belonged to the mill company. In making a new fence Mr. Johnson directed his man, old Richard Hornby, where to plant his trees. Mr. Roughsedge, being informed that the work was an encroachment on the mill land, went to inspect it when Mr. Johnson was not present. Whether there was an argument or not, the two gentlemen got to such high words as to attract the notice of the passers by and some of the mill hands. It was reported that some of the trees in the struggle were pulled up. The affair made a noise in the neighbourhood, but as the matter, whether amicably or not, was settled it soon blew over. If gentlemen and ladies did not show a little of old Adam they would be something more than human.

While writing about Mr. Johnsons old servant, Richard Hornby, one may mention a very generous deed done by the above mentioned Thomas Ellershaw. Both he (Mr. Ellershaw) and his wife, who was blind, were far advanced in life. Richard Hornby and his wife lived in one of Mr. Ellershaw's cottages, which adjoined his own house on the west at the lower end of the village. On account of Mrs. Hornby's faithful nursing, Mr. Ellershaw left to her and her husband a small farm in which a barn, shippon, and other outbuildings stood called Abers. This land adjoined the site of the old bleach house on the Seat Hall estate. The old people were so pleased when the land fell to their lot that they decided to make a portion of the east end of the barn into a small cottage for their own occupation. Here they lived in peace and comfort for many years. As the old couple were identified with the Primitives occasional camp meetings were held in the summer near the house when the congregations were of considerable dimension.

My friend, Christopher Knowles, then of Langcliffe, once tried his hand at public speaking. He little thought then that he would become a Bentham tradesman, and in 1893 the head of Knowles and Sons flourishing grocer and general provisions establishment on the premises where poor Smithers was maddened with drink to the loss of his life.

No.3 (28th October, 1893)

Short Biographical Sketches of the Old Folk of Bentham

Charles Parker

Though I was too young to know much of Charles Parker, only by hearsay, still I well remember the Sunday School for mill girls, which was held in a large room on the north side of Bentham House. The school was under the management of Miss Parker and her governess, who remained in the family as her companion. At the close of the school on Sunday mornings the girls walked in procession, under the direction of the two ladies, to the Cross near the Kings Arms, where the boys from the Church Sunday School joined them on their way to Low Bentham Church. Miss Parker and her companion went with the girls as far as the Church gates, and thence to their own meeting at the Calf Cop on the north side of Low Bentham.

The Parker family, though Quakers, never used their influence to proselytise their workpeople. In winter all the girls were supplied with spencers to keep them warm in going and returning from the Church. At this date Church and Chapel goers never thought it needful for their comfort to have their places of worship made warm with stoves, &c. In connection with Miss Parker's Sunday School, in the winter season there was a night school for sewing, knitting, &c. Many of the mill girls and young women were indebted to these schools for all the education they had the chance of acquiring. When boys and girls were sent to the mill at five or six years of age there was a poor chance for much weekday schooling. For many years after Charles Parker left Bentham his name and family were household words.

Mr. Johnson

Mr. Johnson, after he retired from business, built Grove Hill Mansion. Though he was the wealthiest gentleman in the village, he did not meddle much with either parish or political matters. After a long course of successful business life in London, he evidently wanted to spend the closing years of his life in rural retirement. Mr. Johnson was not only charitable, but he was of such a friendly spirit as to make himself accessible to the poorest of the inhabitants. There was none of that haughtiness of manner and voice which some men showed when a man in humbler position in life dared to ask a favour. He would on occasions sit down in one of the inns with a few working men, treat them with a glass of ale, and chat with them in the most friendly way. He took much interest in the scholars at the Grammar School.

He was long before his day in making a summer outing for the village children. One of this character made a great stir in Bentham when I was about seven or eight years of age. The outing was to Crina Bottom and the top of Ingleborough. Ample provision was made for the occasion, and packed in a cart. On the morning of the holiday all the scholars and their friends had to meet in the large yard at Grove Hill, to be instructed as to their conduct on the way, and put in processional order for marching through the village. Much excitement was caused in passing through the village of Ingleton, for at that day such a gathering for mountain climbing was an unusual thing. The youngest of the scholars, when tired, were taken into the cart in their turn. At Crina Bottom there was a halt for refreshments, after which the youngest part of the company had their choice either to remain where they were to play on the beautiful grass or among the lofty limestone scars, or climb to the top of Ingleborough. Though the day was one of great enjoyment many of us had to wag home with tired limbs.

Mr. Johnson, though a Churchman, took much interest in the Nonconformist bodies. At this early date there was neither church nor chapel in the village. Methodist meetings used to be held, according to my earliest recollection, in the Brown Cow dancing room, and afterwards in that of the Kings Arms. Occasionally the Congregationalists held meetings in the Kings Arms large room. The Rev. Alexander Bell and Mr. Alexander, a lay preacher, and both from the High Street Church, Lancaster, held services occasionally in the same room in an afternoon. Mr. Johnson provided a large number of Watts hymn books for the worshippers. At certain times of the year the Church prayers were read in the lower portion of the Grammar School, and a choir of boys were under the training of the late John Maudsley. Mr. Johnson provided the choir boys with suitable hymn books.

In 1820 a new Methodist chapel was opened at the west end of the village when Mr. Johnson took a pew in the body of that place of worship. It may be of some interest to the Methodists of the present day to be informed that the chapel at that day was called an Armenian Chapel. There is a long history of controversy and bitterness in that word which needs in this article no further explanation. It was usual for Mr. Johnson when there was a collection at the chapel to put a one pound note in the box and a penny on the top of it to weight it. As he had the boys of the

Sunday School on his right he watched their behaviour throughout the service. If any of them were attentive to the preacher he would, at the close of the service, either have spoken to them encouraging words or have invited them to call at Grove Hill after they had taken tea. I and a boy of the name of Joseph Hodgson had a similar invitation for good behaviour when he spoke to us in the kindest manner and gave us some small books and apples.

Some years before his death he was in a feeble state of health and his end came suddenly by an apoplectic attack. The report spread rapidly through the village and much sympathy was felt by the villagers. The funeral was largely attended and many carriages and other conveyances were in attendance. The funeral passed through Bentham about noon and a halt was made at the west end for the arrival of the late Dr. Elletson, Mr. Johnsons nephew, to take part in the funeral procession. As the young gentleman failed to make his appearance the procession slowly wended its way to the Parish Church where the internment took place.

Mr. Roughsedge

Mr. Roughsedge, son of a late vicar of Liverpool, came to Bentham as the successor of Charles Parker. He was of an aristocratic family and bearing, consequently he did not, like Mr. Johnson, show the same friendly disposition towards the common people. He drove his carriage and pair, kept his coachman, footman, and other servants and in position stood higher than any other gentleman, therefore the mill people and the inhabitants generally paid him more homage than any other gentleman. On special occasions at large gatherings he, though not much of a public speaker, would say a few friendly words to the crowd who listened to him. I remember him on one occasion at the close of the old Samaritan Club anniversary, when there was one of the largest gatherings ever seen at the foot of the school hill, speak in friendly words to the members of the society, wishing them prosperity, and to cherish kindly teachings one towards another as men whose interests were one.

There are two things especially which ought to keep the memory of Mr. Roughsedge green. One is the hospice tower which he built on Ingleborough at a very considerable expense. It is true that it was primarily built for a shooting box, but still it was always to remain accessible for the use of the public. It was a strong building with a vaulted roof, with windows and doorway to match. In the centre there was a circular stone table on which shooters and mountain climbers could take their refreshments. As all the materials excepting stone had to be carted up the mountain from the Newby side it may be concluded that the building was reared under exceptionable circumstance. On the opening of it there was a large attendance, exciting races, and much drink poured out to the thirsty ones. It was through this maddening drink that the Hospice Tower soon fell into a mass of ruins. The first night the stone table was broken and other damage done by the roughs which grieved Mr. Roughsedge so much that he lost all interest in it and let it go to ruins. As it is much over sixty years since this event very few persons will remember it.

Happily there is one noble beneficent act in the life of Mr. Roughsedge which will be handed down to remote generations and that is the gift of St. Margaret's Church, High Bentham. This neat church on its lofty site is a great advantage to the Episcopalians of High Bentham and the farmers in the eastern portions of the parish. In my young days people had to go all the way from Mewith Hall, Mewith Head, Burnmoor side, &c., to Low Bentham parish church. It is not too late for the Bentham people to feel grateful to the memory of the man who left them this comfortable church in which to offer Divine worship.

The Wildman Family

An old family of the name of Wildman has some claim to notice. The late William Wildman, whose birthplace was the Helks, near Lowgill in Tatham, was connected with Bentham Methodism some time before the chapel was built in 1820. He was mason, architect, sculptor, &c. In connection with the society he was superintendent of the Sunday school, prayer and class leader, and society steward. He was put on the plan as an exhorter either in 1831 or 1832 during the superintendency of the Rev. Michael Cousins. He was a useful and consistent member of the society, and looked well after the chapel and the various meetings connected with it. Edward, his brother, was a mason, and at times he was a member of the Methodist society, but a rather fickle one. He had a wife who tried him severely, and that in some measure accounted for it.

In addition to his father's trade he was a weaver, a likeness taker by machinery and a village star gazer. He made telescopes, microscopes, and maps of some of the stars. He was also for some time a teacher at a small school in Tatham. He made a velocipede which brought him very much late note. At that time it was called in the village a "*dandy horse*". He on a fine Sunday night exhibited it on a private flat cinder road which lead from the bottom of Gilhead Brow to Gilhead farmhouse. The person who rode the machine propelled it by striking the points of his feet on the ground first on one side of the dandy horse and then on the other. It was remarkable to see such a large number of the villagers and others to witness the trial of such a machine. The youngest brother of the Wildmans was Joseph, and he was a mason and for a time worked at the Methodist Chapel. About the time the mason work was finished he removed to Lancaster, where he spent the remainder of his life. There he joined the Methodist Church at Sulyard street Chapel, and in connection with it he long laboured as a faithful and acceptable local preacher. In the early part of his life in Lancaster he devoted much time to the study of the Hebrew language. In the closing years of his useful life he for some time taught school in a small wooden chapel at Morecambe. This was the first Methodist chapel that was erected at Morecambe. Not a single branch of old Edward Wildman's family has now a name or place at Bentham and its neighbourhood.

Miss Townson and Mrs. Bellman

Mary Townson (Miss), one of the principal general dealers in hats, shoes, &c., and her faithful companion Grace Bellman (Mrs.) were, early in the present century, members of the Methodist Society. For some reason they withdrew from that body and joined the Quakers. For many years they kept up the waning meeting of the Friends at Calfe Cop. In summer and winter, in cold and heat, in storm and calm, the two united Friends might be seen on First day morning on their way to the Meeting House. For a series of years Grace Bellman was the usual speaker. Her addresses though short, were earnest and edifying. Many were the times when these two Friends had to worship with less than half a dozen worshippers. Unhappily they did not live to see the revival of Quakerism in Bentham.

John Barker

John Barker, the postmaster, a churchman, tried in his way to do some good in the village by circulating the Rev. W. C. Wilson's Children's Friend and the Friendly Visitor. He was such an ardent admirer of Mr. Wilson's preaching that he regularly attended the Sunday services at Tunstall Church. He was a member of an old Bentham family, the branches of which have entirely disappeared from the village.

Thomas Holmes

Thomas Holmes was a gentleman considerably advanced in life when he attracted my attention. From what I heard he was for many years the schoolmaster at Wray Grammar School. On leaving Wray he became a principal clerk at Bentham High Mill. On resigning this situation on account of old age, he and his family removed to the shop now occupied by Wm. Greenep. The business was carried on by members of the family, for at this time he was an old man. The Fourlands Farm, that on the road leading to Wennington, was his. He took such a delight in his estate that it appeared to be the solace of his old age. In fine weather it was usual for him to walk to it daily for exercise. The old mans attitude was to walk with his hands behind his back, and to hum in a monotonous voice some ditty that pleased him. In this way he passed on the road without noticing passers by. He appeared, though he was old and bent with the burden of years, to be a very happy old man. Though it must be nearly seventy years since he attracted my attention, his stout frame bent with age, and his hum, hum, are as fresh in my memory as if it had only been of a few years past. A good many years ago his eldest son paid a visit to Bentham, and went over to the Fourlands estate, which he inherited from his father, and while, I think, looking over it was suddenly struck down by death. Not a solitary branch of the happy old mans family remains in the village or neighbourhood.

William Bickerstaff

A good man of the name of Wm. Bickerstaff took my attention before I was ten years of age. He was a Methodist local preacher, and was one of the first teachers in the Wesleyan Sunday School. After spending some years in useful labour in the Settle circuit he removed to Lancaster, where he identified himself with some of the Methodist bodies. For many years he drove the mail cart from Lancaster to Bentham. He was a man widely known and deservedly respected. I believe some of his children still live either at Skerton or Lancaster, and are treading in the good mans steps.

No. 4 (4th November, 1893)

The Origin of the Name of Bentham

A remark on the origin of Bentham may not be without interest. By some it has been said that it is from Benet, a personal name, or from tin or tain, meaning a fire, and having some connection with Ingleborough; others, Benedict, meaning a happy home. It is evident that for many centuries after the compiling of the Domesday Book Bentham was in a district where the land grew little else than rough grass. Bent, a common, a moor called from places being covered with the bent grass. All the allotments or enclosures which were made after the Act for enclosing Bentham moor grew little else but this rough grass. The large allotments extending from Bentham on portions of the east and north-east to Newby Moor and in the direction of Ingleton, Burton-in-Lonsdale, and Ravens Close in my time grew chiefly this grass. Now as A.S. beonet means bent or rough grass, and the A.S. heim or ham an enclosure or home, what looks more likely than that the first Saxons dwelling should be called the home of the bent.

How Bentham Appeared at the Beginning of the Present Century

At this date evidently no new buildings had been put up for several years. The newest were the four cottages in Duck (Duke) street which face the south side of the road leading to the Mill. On the north side in my boyhood there was a number of ash trees, and the enclosure was called Ashgarth. All the other houses, barns, &c., appeared to be of considerable age. At the west end of the village many of the houses are little altered in their appearance. Miss Pattinson's within the Hall yard has been pointed, etc., which has given it a fresher and more modern appearance. The old hall is occupied by Mrs. Shepherd, the oldest lady in the district. She is either 93 or in the 93rd year of her age. She is the widow of the late Robert Shepherd, a branch of an old Chapel-le-Dale family of that name. No one could notice this part of the village without remarking the number of old barns. At the end of the village on the north side the old barn I knew in my boyhood was years ago pulled down and a larger one built on its site. There are still three old barns and shippons, and these and other barns indicate that at one time there was a goodly number of small farmers in the village, many of them no doubt were yeomen living on their own estates.

From the Tweed to the end of the village, which is not more than one-third the length of Bentham, there were twelve barns. The second house on the north side of Bentham coming from the west was at my first recollection occupied by auld Willy Brown, and after him young Willy. When I use auld to the names of old villagers it is not with any disrespect, but it is to show how homely the people were in my youth. The villagers had been brought up to it, and no one took the least offence. It was for a long course of years rented by the late Willy Stephenson, a son of Lawrence Stephenson, and since then it has been occupied by a daughter, Mrs. Hartley, and her husband. At the time the Browns occupied the farm there was a cottage on the west which has been taken down. Adjoining the shippon and the barn that faces up the street and next to the Hall yard was a butching shop. A butcher of the name of Bentham occupied it.

What is now the Horse and Farrier was occupied by its owner, Edward Heaton. It was said that prior to his coming to Bentham he was a gentleman of some importance at Blackburn, and that he was a relation of the Peel family. Though he had been considerably reduced in circumstances he owned the land called Ash Banks and other property. He married the daughter of Parson Benison, head master of the Grammar School, who after his death became the owner of the property. The buildings at this time consisted of the house, barn, shippon, etc. On the other side of the street, and at the west end of Bedlam row, there is a cottage which was used as a small weaving shop. There was no Bedlam row, but two small cottages on its site, occupied by Peter Wilson and Richard Clark, a weaver and shuttlemaker.

Beyond the Horse and Farrier

The next property to these two cottages and gardens was Thomas Ellershaw's. His house had an old-fashioned stone porch, and on the west there was a cottage in which old Richard Hornby lived. Adjoining these there were two old barns with their shippons and stables. At about the centre of them there was an old pig cote which projected into the street, and a middenstead on the high side of it. On the other side of the street there were no houses from what is now the Horse and Farrier on Heaton's property. From here there was a row of seven cottages, which extended to the road leading to the yard and farmhouse now occupied by Mr. A. Brown. Adjoining this was a small cottage, and in the space between it and the house occupied by Mr. Clapham there was a barn, shippons, and other buildings. At the end facing Mr. Clapham's front there was an old hull with a loft above it. Old Clapham Brook, a branch of an old and respectable Bentham family, used to weave sacking in it when he was in a humour to work.

Taking the opposite side of the street, where the Methodist Chapel and School stand, there was nothing but the old pinfold. The Wesleyan property was a part of the Ellershaw estate. On the site of the chapel there were some old ash trees. At this time there were large ash trees on the west, where mountebanks used to fix ropes between them for tightrope dancing. Behind the two barns, etc., there was a large orchard, bounded on the north side with a row of well grown oak trees. It was a custom for villagers to come here for oak branches to hang at the front of their houses on the 29th of May. Between the old pinfold and the premises of Sedgwicks, Lancaster and Settle carriers, there was a small house, which still exists. The stables, barn, and house stood back a considerable distance from the street. The open space was for their large covered carts, etc. On each side of the barn where the goods were stored there were two large dog boxes, one of which was the cot for Tiger and the other for Turk. These two dogs were a terror to both boys and men. It was a custom to let all the horses out into the street on a Sunday morning that they might go to drink at the Tweed water trough. For carriers horses they were very frisky, and as they used to snort, kick, and jump, it was a common saying with timid women when surprised, "*Let me git out t' way, here's Sigwicks' horses i' t' street.*"

On the west of Mr. Seed's house there is a flight of stone steps to a room, which was the principal shoemakers' shop in the country. It was built by the late Isaac Melling at the beginning of this century, and after his death for many years carried on by the late John Leak, his son-in-law. Nearly all the shoemakers in the country were apprenticed at this shop. The last apprentice was Mr. Richard Marsden, who for a long course of years carried on a successful business at Langcliffe. After retiring from business he and his wife removed to Manchester, to spend their last days in quietness. His wife was the third daughter of the late John Wilcock, a branch of an old Bentham family. As Mr. Marsden, who survives her, is over eighty years of age, it must be about 66 years ago. This date marks the decline of the shoemaking trade at Bentham. After Miss Townson (of the shop now occupied by Mr. Wilcock) and other shopmen began to sell imported made shoes, the trade dwindled down to very small dimensions. On the east end of Mr. Seed's house there was a piece of a garden, and as the garden was considerably higher than the street, it was supported by a wall, above which there was a thorn fence. There was no Friends Meeting House or model cottages then, but at the end of the garden there was a cottage occupied by Alice Heaton, the widow of the first Richard Heaton, of Branstane (Brownstone) Beck in Mewith. The adjoining building was a small barn and the next to it was a farmhouse, including a small shoemakers shop, in the possession of John Leak, the older. It was an old thatched house on the west of the Tweed watering trough.

Near the Workhouse

On the west of what was called the New Workhouse was the old Workhouse and a large open square. This large space of ground was used as a playground for boys and girls. Spinning tops, playing at marbles, and shuttlecock were their usual amusements. Blacksmiths hooped cart wheels on it, and caravans and other shows used to stand there. Mountebanks used to perform on the ground when horsemanship was common. The street and every available space in the square was crowded. At this time there were some buildings on the south side, which consisted of a cottage and a large building occupied by the late John Guy as a curriers shop. A family of the name of Nowell lived in a part of it. The Guys were an old Bentham family, and their land was on the low side of Duke-street. The foot-road to Lower Bentham passed through it. It extended to a place in Wenning called Tip teeads (Heads). Tip teeads was a big stone in the deepest part of the river, from which, in bathing time, men and boys went head first into the water. Some one, after this square had been open to the street for hundreds of years, took the liberty of enclosing it with a stone wall.

On the east side of this square was the old poor-house. The front of it did not face the street, but the village playground. It was a long, low, thatched building, and partly in ruins. The first floor was entered by a flight of stone steps, and the three rooms which were considered fit for human dwellings were occupied by poor parishioners. The last persons who occupied them were families of the names of Johnson and Stewart on the first floor, and a widow of the name of Barbara Wilkinson and her two sons in the upper room. John Procter, of Ingleton, married her and placed her in more comfortable circumstances.

The old Workhouse eventually tumbled into ruins, after which it was taken down and the stones were piled up on its site. The building next to the new Workhouse was a smithy, long occupied by old Bob Middlebrook and his three sons, Willy, Jackie, and Hobbie. The adjoining building was an old barn and shippon. This side of the street to as far as Messrs. Knowles' establishment, late Kings Arms Inn, is not much altered in its appearance, except a few shop windows.

King Street

In the Kings Arms yard, now called King-street, there was only one cottage. The stables, &c., were on the west side, the brew-house, dancing-room, &c., on the other side. Between the Kings Arms and Black Bull there was not a single house except Grove Hill (Mr. Johnson's), and Bentham House (Mr. Roughsedge's). On the street side of the Black Bull to the old butching shop, occupied by Mr. Wildman, if there was one cottage, there was not more. The buildings were stables, haylofts, and the public dancing-room. Between here and the old Royal Oak there were two cottages, the one nearest to the public-house belonged to Joss Thornton, and afterwards to his only surviving son, John. Before the Royal was rebuilt there stood a small cottage a little on the east side and close to the street, which was considered an eyesore to the Inn, and was afterwards taken down. From here there were a few houses which extended to the hospital, and also a few on the other side, and this was the extreme east end of old Bentham. Between here and the farmhouse at Lairgill it was pasture and meadow land.

Coming back to Tweed Trough, there were two or three poor dwellings up a narrow passage, occupied by poor people at a low rent. In one there was a family of the name of Arkwright, which brings to ones memory the time when wangby, or blue milk cheese, was a commodity in the grocers shops. This cheese was of such a character that the crust had sometimes to be chopped with an axe. Arkwright managed to scoop out the middle of a large cheese, after which they made a baby-cart of the crust. In this cart to keep their baby quiet or for exercise they used to draw it up and down on the room floor, &c. Wangby cheese making is all but a lost industry.

A little higher up the street where Mr. Procter's shop stands was the village blacksmiths shop. At that time the Middlebrooks occupied it before they went to the smithy at the east end of the new workhouse. Old Bob, as he was always called, was the most noted tale teller in the village. On winter nights young men and boys sat on the smithy hearth or stood around the steady to listen to his tales. While he blew his fire he told the most wonderful tales to his admiring listeners. It was evident that many of his tales were made to suit the occasion. On the site of Mr. Hogg's shop there was an old thatched house. The site of Mrs. Bentham's large shop and house was an old barn and shippon.

In my early boyhood a saddler and his apprentice, Richard Walker, came from Middleham and opened it as a saddlers shop. After Wilson left the village, Richard Walker occupied it for many years. Afterwards it was used as a joiners shop and a tinners shop. The joiner amused the villagers when he advertised ready made coffins. Such a thing had never been heard of before. Passing to the square opposite the Black Bull on the east and north sides there were cottages and the west side was a linen weaving shed.

At the front of the square and a house, for many years occupied by Willy Armistead, there was a wide frontage where stalls were fixed at the Easter and June fairs, and earthenware and other ware were exposed for sale. At the east end of this open space there was an old barn running from south to north. Its gable end bound the street and against it was fixed a milestone 15 miles to Lancaster. As it has disappeared, what has become of it? There was not a single house up Robin-lane excepting Low Bankhead.

Crossing over to the school hill there were two cottages on the west of the school belonging to Melling's Butterber farm and two cottages on the east of the school, one occupied by Michael Slinger and the other by Neddy Wildman the younger. From here there was not another house, with the exception of Lairgill, for half a mile or more, and that was Fowgill. The school hill was an open playground to the little stream which runs by Lairgill old farm house, which is now in ruins. It may be interesting to the Wesleyans to learn that this was a Methodist preaching place towards the close of the last century. It would be interesting to learn whether this large portion of waste ground (school hill) was enclosed by an Act of Parliament or by some irresponsible parochial authority. Persons who have looked over the award of the enclosure of the Bentham Moor know that certain lands were left for public use, such as Wennington Moss, Linga Cross for sand, for bull land at Nutgill, which appears to be lost.

MRS. A. BENTHAM
MILLINER, DRESSMAKER, AND DRAPER,
BENTHAM.
Has returned from Town with

Novelties in Spring Goods.
MILINERY, MANTLES, AND JACKETS, DRESS
MATERIALS, FANCY GOODS, ETC.
Experienced Dressmakers and Milliners on the Premises.

No.5 (18th November, 1893)

The Road from Low Bentham to High Bentham in 1893

It is somewhat remarkable that High and Low Bentham are very little nearer each other than they were 200 years ago. The farm house on the east side of Ellerbeck, Low Bentham, was the nearest house to High Bentham in 1819, and it was occupied by a farmer of the name of Ellershaw, who carried on shoemaking. In 1820 John Davidson built two neat cottages at a short distance nearer High Bentham than the farm house, so that the two villages stand as to distance as they did seventy-two years ago. On the way to High Bentham a small farm house was made out of a portion of Longlands barn. At about the middle way between the villages, when I was a boy, Richard Marshall bought a small field, I believe, of Parson Butler, the Rector of Bentham, on which he built a dwelling house and made a market garden. It is still occupied by one of his family.

The next building, which is on the opposite side of the road, is an old building called Burrow Barn. In my youth it was a haunted barn and it was always dreaded by children when they had to pass it in the dark. On such occasions boys always, to keep up their courage, either whistled or set off on a run, until they were some distance beyond it. The flaings, as they were termed, were of dwarfish stature, and they used to play their midnight pranks in a small carriage on the Chitty baulks. A man of the name of Will Clarke told me that one night when he was passing the barn in the dark he saw a clergyman of a neighbouring parish about to meet him when he shot out with frightful suddenness into a flame of fire and passed through a tall thorn fence on the opposite side of the barn. The thorns crackled as if they were on fire. On another occasion he saw the boggart in another form, when it crossed the road and disappeared in the dark through a hole in the dyke. One dark night he and I were coming from visiting a sick boy at Low Bentham. I noticed before we reached the barn he ceased for some time to speak. Asking the reason for his long silence, he said, "*I saw a coffin cross the road.*" The boy died during the night. This might be mere imagination, but this I can vouch from the mans character that to him it was real and that he was not a person that would tell a deliberate lie.

Not far from the barn is Moons Acre, on which John Titterington built a good house and malt kiln. The old malt kiln was on the west side at the entrance of Low Bentham, originally in the possession of the late Mr. Ellershaw, and for many years under the management of his son-in-law, the founder of the new malting industry. In the course of a few years he added to his business that of a spirit merchant. After the premises came into the hands of the Collingwood Trust, a new school was built, to which the head master and his scholars were removed from the Bentham school. On the opposite side of these premises Mr. Whittaker has built a substantial dwelling house and made a large market garden. At a short distance from Moons Acre, and a little out of Upper Bentham, the Primitives many years ago built a new Chapel, to serve the members of the two villages. Through some neglect of the principal leaders, the cause went down, and as there was no prospect of a revival, the chapel was made into a house, which is now occupied by Mr. Thomas Knowles, of the firm of Knowles and Sons. Since that time adjoining this a neat and substantial Roman Catholic day school has been built.

In coming into Bentham, to avoid confusion, it will be an advantage to take the buildings on the south side of the street.

Bentham in 1893: The South Side of Main Street

There have been very few new houses built in Bentham as it appeared in my boyhood, and the chief additions in this respect have been built out of old barns or on the site of barns. Over 60 years ago a house and shop was made of some portion of Mr. Heaton's house, and it was here where the late Henry Carr began his successful grocery business. Some time ago this house and shop were added to the Horse and Farrier. A cottage has been made out of the barn on the west of the hostelry, and is now in the occupation of the family of the late Mr. Stephenson. A little higher up at the east end of Heaton's property a cottage was built more than half a century ago, and at that time occupied by Peter Nicholson. For a considerable course of years it has been the residence of Anthony Alderson, a branch of an old Dent family, who removed to Bentham in my early days. A house has been added to the row of houses on the high side of this cottage. From what I have heard this, and some adjoining house or houses, is in the hands of a branch of old Michael Slinger's family. A little higher up the street there is a thoroughfare to some back premises where a small barn has been made into a cottage. Next to the farm house of Anthony Brown there is a small cottage, on the high side of which there is a row of fine cottages made of barn buildings and shippons.

A new house nearly seventy years ago was made at the east end of John Skirrow's residence and is on the right leading to Tennants Well. It was first occupied by the late Wm. Wildman, and afterwards by William Jackman, slater and plasterer, from Langcliffe. By his industry and thrift he laid the foundation of a good business now carried on successfully by his sons. A cottage has been made where the old hat shop stood. On the west side of the site of the old poorhouse, and on the south side of the old village playground, three or four houses have been made on the site, &c., of Guys old curriers shop. Over sixty years ago the small house at the east end was a shoemakers shop occupied by Tom Faraday, the leader of Bentham Band.

On the site of the old poorhouse two good shops have been built, one of which is a greengrocer's shop and the other a grocer and stationer's shop. After the paupers were removed from the new poorhouse to Giggleswick Workhouse, it was turned into a beerhouse, after which it was rented for the sale of wares of useful articles. When it was occupied by C. Knowles it was used as a grocers shop, temperance hotel, &c. After an occupancy by Mr. John Quinlan, it was made into a dwelling house and shop. The smithy, so long occupied by the Middlebrooks, Robinsons, and Howsons, has been made into a storeroom for the adjoining ironmongers shop. This large shop and house, which are in the occupancy of Mr. Howson, were built on the site of an old barn and shippon.

The Kings Arms

Great improvements have been made in the premises of the Inn, for many years known as the Kings Arms, since it was sold by Mr. Atkinson, the last of the landlords, to Mr. John Rice, of Grove Hill. After it came into the possession of Mr. Rice, Mr. C. Knowles rented it as a grocer's shop, temperance hotel, &c. Mr. Rice made some improvements fronting the Mill-lane, before he sold it to Mr. Knowles. The improvements in the Inn yard, on the west side, now known as King-street, were made to perpetuate the name of the Old Hostelry. The old cottage, stables, and hayloft, on the east side of this street were purchased by the late Mr. Richard Butterfield, who made them into cottages. Their present owner is Mr. William Greenep, who lets two of them for a liberal clubroom, &c. Partly behind these cottages Mr. Greenep has built a workshop and warehouse to meet the requirements of his own increasing business. On the opposite side of King-street Mr. Knowles has made the old brewhouse into the dancing room, and the adjoining stables into business premises. On the vacant plot of ground adjoining, a warehouse, well cellared and three storeys high, has been built for salting and drying bacon. The various branches of Mr. Knowles' industry have increased to such an extent that the whole premises are now one lock-up shop. Near the warehouse a new cottage has been built for one of the workmen.

On the west side of the Mill-lane, adjoining the Kings Arms, the late Mr. Atkinson built a large public room which was used as a dancing room and for other purposes. At one time it was used by the Free Methodists for religious services on Sunday afternoons, and by the Friends in the evening for bible readings. This room has been made for business purposes. The house occupied by Mr. R. Sanderson fills the space which was used as a thoroughfare to the old brewery, dancing room, and the back parts of the public room mentioned above. That room with an altered frontage has been made into a draper's shop now occupied by Mr. Sanderson, a hairdresser's shop by Mr. E. Jackman, and a watchmaker's shop by Mr. F. Hind. The two latter premises are lock-up shops, and the rooms above are occupied by Mrs. Sanderson for millinery and dressmaking and show room. The two adjoining better class houses were built more than fifty years ago, one of which is now the post office. At a short distance on the north side of the station, Mr. Francis Holmes has built himself a plumber and tinners shop and a good dwelling house. A little on the west, where there were barn, stables, and shippon, two cottages have been built out of some of them.

At a little distance southward stands the vicarage occupied by the vicar, the Rev. J. L. Holbeck. Formerly the land on this side of the station was a part of the Grove Hill estate. The house occupied by Mr. Holbeck was built by the late Mr. Langstreth, many years landlord of the Kings Arms, as an hotel for the accommodation of railway travellers. At a considerable distance on the west of the Vicarage are the gasworks which were built in 1862.

Procters Corn Mill

On the opposite side of the railway station there are four better class houses called South View, which were built by Mr. James Procter, jun. On the west of these houses and partly in line with them Mr. Procter built a corn mill in 1880, which, on account of increasing business, was enlarged in 1883, and again in 1893. The area of the site of the mill is about 300 yards, and that of the warehouse 230 yards. The plant is one of the best in the district, as the machinery is of the latest improvements and the best construction, so that work can be done with remarkable quickness. The machinery is adapted for cleaning oats and making them into meal, and also for grinding provender and feeding stuffs. The staple trade is making meal, four loads of which can be ground per hour, and twenty sacks of provender in the same time. There is also a small saw-mill run for hire, every mechanical facility is provided for loading and unloading. From a railway siding 230 sacks can be delivered into the mill or warehouse per hour. Coal is shunted to the side of the boiler so it can be discharged with quick despatch. The industry which employs five or six men is of great service to Bentham and its neighbourhood.

Returning from the station on the north side of Grove Hills large gates there are three excellent shops, the first of which is the Co-operative, the next Mr. Smith's barber's shop, and Mr. W. Phillipson's watchmaker's shop. Adjoining this shop is the new Public Hall consisting of market house, reading room, large assembly room, &c.

The large premises on the north side of the Public Hall are the old Black Bull Inn, which have been largely improved by Mr. Coates, the present landlord. Formerly there were on the south side a garden and a small croft adjoining Grove Hill ground: A deal of this space has been taken up with stables, coach-house, and other buildings. Great improvements have been made in the interior of the Inn for the accommodation of travellers. On the north side of the premises, where there used to be stables, haylofts, and a thoroughfare under the old dancing room, now there are Mr. Foster's greengrocer's shop, Mr. Parkinson's shoe and saddler's shop, and Mr. Irvine's clogger's shop. A new slaughter-house has been built behind the old butching shop occupied by Mr. Wildman. Formerly the animals were slaughtered in the butching shop, as the name implies. In my boyhood days there was a house adjoining the Royal Oak, occupied and owned by Joss Thornton. This has been made into two cottages.

The Royal Oak was rebuilt by the Burrows, of Guy Hill, and some years afterwards it was purchased by John Clapham, of Green Smithy, Mewith. Many years ago it was purchased by Mr. Leeming, the landlord, and he built a large market room and other buildings. On the east of this Inn there is a row of houses, the first of which Mrs. Thompson (maiden name Easterby) built after the death of her husband for her own dwelling. On the other side of the hospital there were one or two cottages in 1817. The number has been increased. Further east there is a large house called Mount Pleasant, occupied by Mr. R. Wilcock, grocer. It was built when I was a lad at school by the late Richard Wray, of Mewith. He was a flour dealer, and used to do business in the village. Establishing a good business he built Mount Pleasant, which was fitted up for the wholesale and retail business.

Further east Mr. Thompson, solicitor, has built a good house, with offices, etc. Nearby the late Mr. William Titterington built a good house, which is occupied by Mrs. Titterington. On the east there are another two houses of a better class. On this side of the street, over fifty years ago, the late W. Wildman built two small cottages, which Mrs. Wildman sold to the late Mr. Titterington after her husbands death. The houses above mentioned are the extent of Bentham on the south side.

T. MARSHALL,
COMPLETE HOUSE FURNISHER,
AND BEDDING WAREHOUSEMAN,
BENTHAM.
Plain and Artistic Furniture made to any design.
Carpets, Linoleums, Oilcloths, etc

MARSHALL'S, BENTHAM

No.6 (25th November, 1893)

The Improvements on the North Side of Old Bentham

The structural improvements made on this side of Bentham since 1817 have given the village a more respectable and modern appearance. Many old barns, shippons, and other old buildings have either been made into cottages and shops, or pulled down to make sites for structures of a more valuable and useful character. The fourth house from the west end, seventy years ago was a weaving shop. At that time it was not unusual for people in good circumstances to weave and do other light manual labour. In this shop a gentlemans son, who had been a soldier, did a little work to furnish himself with pocket money. Clapham Brook, a member of a well-to-do old Bentham family, did a little weaving for the same thing. At that time some of the better class of people did not think it beneath them to do a little work in their homes for the mill company. Women who could live, as it is said, without work, made meal sacks at one shilling a dozen, the mill company finding the tarry twine. Some of them were not ashamed of wheeling them, when made, in a barrow to the mill warehouse.

Young women, daughters of leading tradesmen, yea, some of them men of landed property, were allowed, shortly after the mill company started business, to work a portion of their time in the mill for pocket money. A son of a gentleman of landed property, who intended his second son to be a solicitor, was sent to an office at Settle. After a short service he made up his mind to return to his fathers to be apprenticed with the mill company to a flax-dressing business. At that time it was considered a business fit for a gentlemans son. Over fifty years ago I met with an independent gentleman near Fleetwood who told me that when he was a young man he dressed hemp at Bentham mill, and at that time he and the other men made ten shillings a day. As a matter of course that was in the days of our great grandfathers and grandmothers, but now it would be such a lowering in modern society that few well-to-do persons would stoop to touch the tarry twine, throw a shuttle, or associate with mill hands.

Scotland-Row (Bedlam)

The row of cottages now called Scotland-row was built about seventy years ago by the Mill Company for their work people when sailcloth weaving was introduced into the village. The basement or ground floor was a weaving shed. When the sailcloth trade went down the shed was made into cottages. Above the shed there were twelve dwellings, consisting of two rooms for each family. Its original name was Bedlam, and it is sometimes called by this name now. The origin of it was this, when the building was covered in and the joiners began to put in the joists &c., as the whole length of the building was left open on Sundays for many weeks, the boys and girls of the village made the place their playground. They shouted, yelled, and screamed to such an extent that the neighbours, who considered it a nuisance, said it was worse than Bedlam. As Kirkham-row, now called Lairgill row, was built for sailcloth weaving, it may be mentioned in connection with Bedlam.

I was a very little boy when the row of sixteen houses was made. There was a cellar in each house to hold four looms for sailcloth weaving. The origin of New Kirkham was this: The Mill Company of Hornby, &c., before the two rows of house were constructed, their sailcloth trade was carried on at Kirkham in Lancashire. As a matter of course the sailcloth weavers and their families were then removed to Bentham. Under the circumstances it was only reasonable for them to call their new houses Kirkham, to keep in memory the homes they had left. It was the usual thing for the village boys to quarrel with the New Kirkham boys at school and to say provoking things to one another. They used to shout the following doggerel rhyme: "*Kirkhamites, Kirkhamites. lapped up in a pen, darn't turn out to Yorkshire men*". The challenge was thrown back with the response: "*Yorkshirebites, Yorkshirebites, lapped up in a pen, darn't turn out to Lancashire men*".

On the east of Bedlam there is a row of five houses, some of which were made out of two old barns, shippons, stables, &c. One is a grocer's shop long occupied by the late Henry Carr and Sons, and now occupied by Mrs. Jackson. A little eastward is the Wesleyan Chapel built in 1820, and partly rebuilt and greatly enlarged a few years ago. The Sunday School adjoining was built on the site of the old pinfold. The next dwelling is a cottage which was recently bought by the chapel trustees and somewhat enlarged and made more convenient, which is occupied by Mr. R. Bush, draper, &c. This was one of the few houses, over seventy years ago, in which a loom for weaving sacking was put up. Willy Smith was the weaver, and he and his wife Molly were two of the most inoffensive couples in the village. For a long course of years he, on account of feeble health, was on the sick list of the Samaritan Club. A rather laughable occurrence took place which showed the influence of superstition. He was much given to walking in the fields, and one Sunday morning he walked to Seat Hall Farm. As hazel trees were common in the fences he thought, though it was Sunday, that there would be no harm in gathering a few nuts. While thus engaged he, to reach a bough, caused too much tension on his braces when all the four buttons flew off. He was so alarmed thinking it was a judgement from heaven for Sabbath desecration, that he started for home at a quicker pace than usual. Perhaps it would be no worse for society if such superstition was a little more common, so as to prevent some people from doing worse things than gathering a handful of nuts on a Sunday. A very sad event happened to this aged and happy couple, which evoked widespread sympathy and caused a general sorrow in the neighbourhood. Lingering in feebleness some years after the event narrated, Willy Smith died, which affected his wife very much and made her feel her loneliness keenly. The day when he died a kind neighbour persuaded her to stay the night with her family. Though she felt doubly distressed, she could not be persuaded to stay another night from her dead husband. In the morning her good Samaritan entered the house to look after the wants of the stricken one, when, to her horror, she found her dead beside her husband. The report quickly spread through the village, and the sorrow for the double death was widespread. As the deceased were loving and peaceable in their long married life, and could not in death be parted, they were both buried on the same day and in the same grave at Low Bentham Church. For deep solemnity and impressiveness it was one of the most affecting funerals which ever took place at Bentham.

A little eastward, in the open space where Sedgwicks kept their carriers carts, &c., there are a house and a grocer and general dealers shop occupied by Mr. Morphet. Partly behind these premises Mr. Lamb has a cabinet shop. On the high side of Mr. Seed's cabinet shop, where there used to be a garden, cottage, and barn, there are now the Friends Meeting-house and School behind, and Grove Cottages. The three cottages, which were built by the late Mr. Rice, are model structures and of an attractive design. Adjoining are Mr. T. Marshall's premises, built on the site of an old thatched farm house. His cabinet shop, warehouse, and showrooms are all constructed on a good plan for carrying on a successful and interesting business. Between Mr. Marshalls premises and the houses, a little eastwards, there is a thoroughfare to a narrow street called Tweed-street. Formerly there were two old dilapidated hovels, now Mr. Coulam has three superior cottages and Mr. Jackman six of a similar character. Attached to some of the cottages, if not the whole of them, there are neat and well-cultivated gardens.

Ascending eastward there is Mr. Procter's (*"The Beehive"*), a drapers shop, and from its name one of general business activity. It is built on the site of the ancient village smithy, long occupied by Robert Middlebrook and Sons before they removed to the smithy at the east end of the Workhouse. It must be between sixty and seventy years since it was purchased by the late Robert Ward and made into a general wholesale and retail drapers shop. After he retired from business, for a long course of years it was carried on by Mr. Quinlan, who married Rachel, Mr. Wards eldest daughter. Miss Ward was a young woman of clever business habits and before she was out of her teens she did much business for her father at Manchester. Some years after her husbands death she made over the business to her oldest son, and purchased some old cottages in the main street, Ingleton, and built on their site one of the best and largest drapers shops either in the village or district - good business was done and it is now carried on by Mr. S. Leach.

Middlebrook Family

It may be of some interest to know what became of the old village blacksmiths family of Middlebrooks. After the old man died it was said Jacky and Hobbie went to Preston, and Willy, who remained in the parish, opened a blacksmiths shop a little above Greensmithy, in Mewith. Willy was a very quiet sort of a man, but he had a way of doing many things different to anybody else. For instance, before he would order his iron to be sent by the carrier he would take his turf barrow and go fourteen miles or more to Lancaster for it and wheel it all the way back. He carried out the same plan in getting a supply of coals for his smithy and domestic use. He took his favourite barrow and jogged cheerfully on his way to Ingleton colliery, a distance of four or five miles for his coal. In his old age he came into possession of one of Collingwood's hospital cottages at High Bentham. He had always been very fond of a game cock and he cherished that affection in his extreme old age. It is said that in his hospital cottage he kept one or two of his favourite birds in a cupboard.

Mr. Hogg's draper's shop is built on the site of a very old thatched house, which was built by a masterman nailer, of the name of Blackburn. Eventually he sold it, and with his wife emigrated to America, where in course of time he was made a magistrate. Beyond Mr. Hoggs from time immemorial there were four cottages, a barn, and a shippon. After Mr. Robert Jackson bought the property, which belonged to an old Bentham family of the name of Guy, he made the barn and shippon into a good dwelling house, and a large shop for the grocery and general business. It is now in the possession of Mrs. Bentham, who carries on the drapery and millinery business. Great structural improvements have been made on the south side of the square. There was a large open space to the street where pottery and other wares used to be exposed for sale at fairs and on market days. There is now a tailors and drapers shop kept by Mr. Garlick. The old linen weaving shed on the west side in the square has been made into cottages. Further eastward, where there was an old thatched barn in ruins, there are a fancy and dressmaking shop kept by Miss Maudsley, and a cooks shop kept by Mr. Vipond. The barn was made into shops with their dwelling houses by Mr. Gorrill.

School Hill

At the turn into Robbin Lane, Mr. Wilson has built two good houses and a warehouse, &c., for the sale of fents and carrying on the tailor and drapery business. A little further up the lane Mr. W. Coates has built a good house and appendages connected with the building trade. An open space between Mr. Wilson's and Mr. Coates' has been purchased for a Church of England Sunday School and class rooms. Near these buildings and on the low side of the school there were two cottages, once connected with the Butterber estate, made into one. The Collingwood School was lengthened over sixty years ago, so that now the west end joins the gable end of the double cottage. On the north side of the school some class rooms have been built against it. On the east side of the school over seventy years ago there were two cottages, and this was the end of old Bentham. The two cottages had looms in them for occasional weaving. One occupant was a slater and plasterer, and as work was all but nil in the winter he had to weave to supplement his livelihood. The other occupant had several trades, and he used to weave when work was scarce.

It was recently said in the Lancaster Guardian that sixty or seventy years ago there was a loom in nearly every house in Bentham. This statement was made no doubt from wrong information. In this article I have mentioned three houses which at one time had looms in them. A year or two ago I spoke to a cousin of mine who lived twelve years in Bentham before I was born, and she had no recollection of any house having a loom in it. The houses in Kirkham-row were cellared for looms, so there was no need for looms in their houses. It is very likely before Bentham mill was built, which would be in the second half of the last century, there would be a good deal of cotton weaving in houses same as there was at Burton-in-Lonsdale, Ingleton, and other neighbouring villages.

The addition made to old Bentham on the School hill by building a superior class of houses is a great improvement. Where there were two old houses a new age has been added to them. Coming near the street there is a new saddlers shop and houses occupied by Mr. John Willan. On the top of the School hill there are four excellent houses with a nice frontage for flowers which were built by the late John Slinger, a descendant of two old Bentham families. Opposite Mount Pleasant an occupation road to Butterber pastures divides the houses on the School hill. On the east side of the road there are houses of a better class, one of which is the residence of Mr. Geo. Sedgwick, the present owner of Butterber farm. I believe the name of the house is Butterber. This farm for a long series of years was in the possession of one of the oldest Bentham families. In the reign of Richard II, 1379, there was a John Melling in the neighbourhood who paid the poll tax. Before Bentham Moor was enclosed Butterber was the boundary farm on the north side of the village, and most of the land between it to a short distance on the south side of Ingleton was open moor. The new house on the east of Butterber is the Manse or parsonage for the second minister in the Settle Wesleyan Circuit. Some one who took a fancy to a Hebrew name called it "*Beulah*". As the word named means "*married*", or rather "*thou art married*", Bishop Lowth renders it "*thy land shall be married*". Though the name might be given on account of the dominating landscape views which surround it, still that does not make out the word Beulah. Beyond Kirkham-row, Mr. James Bibby has recently built a very substantial and convenient house in an allotment through which there is a footway to Ingleton. Its name is Asperlands, no doubt from the name of the land on which it is built.

This field reminds one of an event which took place over seventy years ago. At the time the fighting craze was strongly developed through the district, and it was seldom that parish constables did much to check fighting. The occurrence was a pitched battle for one sovereign. One of the combatants was an Ingleton collier named Jimmy Lowther, but the name of his opponent has passed from my recollection. As the public generally liked to see a good battle, there was a large crowd. The two men, with their backers, arrived at the fixed time, to the delight of the sightseers, who were impatient to see science, as it was termed, or English pluck. After stripping to their shirts they fixed themselves in the pugilistic position, after which they shook hands, before the sign was given to start. After they had pummelled one another for about an hour the battle ended with a shake of hands, and the brutal affair was discussed before and against the combatants.

The New Houses in Robbin Lane

There are four main road entrances to Bentham, and it is rather singular that the village has extended in every direction but the west. Indeed, what was the last house in 1817 was taken down very many years ago. All the new houses in Robbin-lane and in the direction of Ingleton are of a very good class of dwellings. The first new buildings on the right are the girls and infant schools. They are substantial buildings, and their architectural appearance shows well. The two good houses on the north were built by Dr. Bradley, one of which was lately sold to Mr. Wm. Knowles, which he has occupied since the old Kings Arms was made a lock-up shop. Near the turn in the road there are the priests house, the Roman Catholic Chapel, and a cottage on the opposite side of the road, made from a portion of Butterber barn. The priests house was made when I was in my young manhood by a man of the name of Shepherd, on his leaving as landlord of the Brown Cow. After his death, Mrs. Charnley in her widowhood, after retiring from the Black Bull, occupied it as a beer house. Low Bankhead, now Bank-view, has been very much enlarged and improved. When I was a lad a robbery was committed there, but the thief was never found out.

On the east at Butts Lane Head, the late Mr. Robertshaw built two houses of a better class. Indeed all the houses in this direction are of a similar character. At a short distance on the same side of the road there are three houses with nice flower gardens in front, belonging to Messrs. Gorrill, Hind, and Rhodes. A little higher up the road there are two houses of a similar character, facing the south-east. The views all around command Ingleborough, Burnmoor, Tatham Fells, &c. On the south of Highbank Head Mrs. E. Holmes is building two superior houses, on a site surpassing all those mentioned for varied and extensive views. The views in every direction embrace mountain and valley scenery in the northern division of the West Riding of Yorkshire, Lancashire, Westmorland and Cumberland.

BENTHAM.
J. T. WHITTAKER,
GARDENER AND SEEDSMAN, BENTHAM,
Agent for H. RICHARDSON & Co, Manure Merchants, York.

ALL MANURES requisite for Farm and Garden. Basic Slag, Rape Dust, Phosphates, Ground Bones (all sizes) All Manures guaranteed. Prices on application. (1620

No. 7 (9th December, 1893)

The Tradesmen of Bentham: Collapsed and New Industries

Considering the great falling off of staple industries which were at their best fifty or sixty years ago, it is remarkable how a village so small at that date has risen to its present dimensions by the local trade. If the present tradesmen and their various crafts are compared with those of 1820, which have already been mentioned in these reminiscences, it will be seen how greatly the local trade has been extended. There are fourteen shops on the north side of Bentham, where there were none in 1820, and eleven of them are new structures. On the south side there are sixteen shops, where there were none at the same date, and ten of them are new structures. In 1820 Mr. Holmes' place was a grocer's shop, Mr. W. Greenep's was the same, and Mr. Seed's was a grocer's shop. The house where Mr. R. Smith lives was a shop for flour and oatmeal. The old house on the east side of Mr. Hogg's was old Nancy Swithenbank's bakehouse and gingerbread shop. The house on the other side of the street and opposite to Mrs. Bentham's was a shop for clogs, pattens, etc. Mr. Wilcock's shop was the co-operative shop, and that on its west was a grocer's shop. There were a few small shops which need not be mentioned.

Professional Gentlemen and Tradesmen

Vicar, Rev. J. L. Holbeck. Medical men, Drs. Metcalfe, Bradley, and Griffiths. Solicitors, Messrs. H. J. J. Thompson and G. S. Tatham. Schoolmasters and schoolmistresses, Mr. J. Llewellyn, B.A., headmaster of the Grammar School; Mr. Wilson Hewitt, headmaster of elementary schools; Mr. J. D. Hewitt, assistant master; Miss Band, headmistress of the Girls School; Miss Fletcher, second mistress; Miss Harrison, Miss Atkinson, and Miss Bottomley, assistants. Miss Wilson, private school. The Bentham Hemp Spinning Company, Bentham Gas Company. Grocers and general dealers, Messrs. Knowles and Sons, Messrs. Wilcock and Sons, Co-operative Association, Messrs. B. Holmes, J. Harker, T. Morphet, and Mrs. Jackson. Drapers, &c., Messrs. H. Hogg, T. Procter, J. Hemmingway, G. W. Garlick, R. Sanderson, R. Bush, R. Wilson, Mrs. Bentham, and Miss Maudsley.

Greengrocers, T. Foster, A. Bibby. Watchmakers, Messrs. W. Phillipson, F. Hind, C. Holmes, and W. J. Phillipson. Cabinetmakers and carpenters, Messrs. T. Marshall, J. Seed, W. Lamb, W. Caverley, Exors, Cumberland. Slaters and plasterers, Messrs. J. Jackman & Sons, Mr. H. Slinger. Hairdressers and tobacconists, Mr. R. Jackman and Mr. F. Smith. Shoemakers and cloggers, Messrs. R. Smith, R. Parrington, J. Irvine, W. Burrow, H. Procter. Saddlers, Messrs. I. Willan and R. Parrington. Auctioneer, Mr. R. Turner. Plumbers, tinmen and painters, Messrs. F. Holmes, W. Greenep, R. Robinson. Tailors, Messrs. S. Auton, T. Bowker, I. Hutchinson, I. Shepherd, T. Wilcock, I. Bibby, and I. Stephenson. Leather merchant, Mr. R. Greenep. Veterinary surgeon, Mr. E. Holdsworth. Cornmiller, etc., Mr. J. Procter, jnr. Butchers, Messrs. I. Wildman, J. C. Clapham, R. Kidd, W. Townley.

Innkeepers, Royal Oak, Mr. R. Bottomley; Black Bull, Mr. A. Coates; Brown Cow, Mrs. Alderson; Horse and Farrier, Mrs. Cooper. Beerhouse, Mr. W. Robinson. Masons, Mr. W. Coates, Messrs. Cumberland.

Industries Which Have Callapsed

Considering the number of important industries which have gone down within the last forty or fifty years, it is very remarkable how Bentham has not only sustained the shock, but under the untoward circumstances has grown to its present dimensions.

The Weaving Trade

Linen weaving was a very important business, and a large number of men were constantly employed in it. There was a large weaving shed on the west side of the mill premises, with its entrance on the south near the river Wenning. In my youth a large number of men found constant employment in this shed. There was a long weaving shed on the west side of the square which gave employment to a number of men. There was a small weaving shop on the high side of Wenning Bridge at Low Bentham where the same trade was carried on in connection with the High Bentham mill. There was a little weaving done by a man who lived at Tenant House at a distance of a mile on the Clapham-road. A man of the name of Roger Carr did a little weaving in a small place near the ruins of the old Poor-house. Some of the cleverest workmen in this industry were employed in the tablecloth weaving. This industry, which gave employ- ment to a large number of families has entirely disappeared.

Sailcloth Weaving

This important industry, which was transferred from Kirkham to Bentham, over seventy years ago, by Hornby and Company, is a thing of the past. The large shed on the base of Bedlam was filled with two rows of looms to meet the requirements of the trade. Some idea may be formed of the extent of the trade when it is stated that at New Kirkham, where there are sixteen houses, there were four looms in each cellar, sufficient to employ sixty-four weavers. This trade, which began to wane about 1830, like the linen trade, has gone down. The sack cloth, or what is called locally "*harden*" weaving, was a very brisk trade over sixty years ago. This work was chiefly done by the small farmers in Mewith. Very little was done at Bentham. This added considerably to the livelihood of the farmers, as it was work they could attend to in wet weather, in summer, or hay-time. There was a fixed day for taking in or out, and it was a time of no ordinary activity. The farmers came down from the hills with their little horses and carts filled with their web or pieces for delivery at the warehouse. What with the delivery and taking out weft and warps, Mr. Thomas Winder, the foreman, and his men had a busy day. Very few of the villagers of Bentham can have any idea of the stirring times at the mill warehouse when the linen, sailcloth, and sackcloth weavers delivered their work and took out work to be done. Carts, barrows, &c., were utilised for the traffic, and the mill land and Mewith roads were thronged with workmen. Now all that has passed away and it is likely that the rattle of the shuttle, the beat of the beam, and the noise of the treadles are silenced for ever. With the weaving of sacking, the making of sacks has been lost to Bentham.

The Flax Dressing Trade

This industry, which in the first half of the present century, was brisk, is now a thing of the past. There were three long shops, with double berths outside the mill, and a small one on the south, which was used when there was a push in the business. In addition to these shops there were two hackling machine shops in a building which projected westward from the spinning mill, and they were worked by a mill-race connected with the Wenning. The ground floor shops were filled with machines, but the one above it was not more than half filled: These machines were generally called Solomons, either from the inventor or the man who introduced them to the mill.

In the wreck of industries that of bleaching occupies no mean place. The business was of great importance, and was extensive down to about ten or twelve years ago. This industry, when first started, was of very small dimensions. The works, which were erected on the north side of a small stream on Seat Hall estate, and close to a foot way leading from the west end of Bentham to Burton-in-Lonsdale, were nearly a mile away from the mill. When these works were removed to a large site on the north side of the river Wenning, and on the west of the high mill, the disused building was made into three cottages. When these cottages failed to gain occupants, they were taken down and the old material used for other purposes. The new bleach works were on a large scale, and gave employment to a large number of men.

The outside work was very trying for the bleachers, especially in winter. It was enough to break down the health of the most robust men. Indeed some of them who entered the business when they were beyond their teens became incurable cripples through rheumatism. Under a large shed open to the south there were a number of pits, through which a stream of water passed from a mill-race into Wenning. On each side of those pits there was machinery for wringing the wetted yarn by the hand. The men stood beside their pits on flags, without shoes and stockings, their trousers rolled above their knees, and their shirt sleeves rolled up above the elbows. In this position they took the yarn, dipping it and working it about in the water, and then adroitly throwing it on a crook to be wrung as dry as possible. This work went on from early morn to night, summer and winter, from boyhood to the grave, and all for a very small wage. Happily this mode of bleaching is a thing of the past. In the heyday of this business the field on the west of the works used to be white with the linen yarns, either spread on the grass or on the poles.

There was a large field on the low side of High Botton used in the same way for bleaching purposes. As it was on the opposite side of the Wenning to the bleaching-house, the two places were connected by a wooden bridge, which was taken down when the trade began to decline. The only bleaching done now is done by four or five hands within the mill, under the management of Mr. Smith.

When I was about eight or nine years of age, the manager of the bleachworks was Sam Evans, who was not of an old Bentham family. He was of the habit of drinking freely at the end of the week. One dark Saturday night he was so drunk and confused when he got to the bottom of the village that instead of going to his home at the Mill, he wandered on the way to Low Bentham, until he met with a terrible fright from what he called a boggart, or the village dobbie. The fright affected him for good, more than all sermons he had ever heard at either church or chapel, so that he became a new man and joined in fellowship with the Methodists. From his reformed and general good conduct he shortly won the office of Superintendent of the Sunday School. Though I was of but tender years his solemn looks, earnest prayers, and his exhortations to the children to fear God, speak the truth, be obedient to parents, and kind to one another, are still fresh in my memory. Whether there are such nocturnal beings as boggarts or not the thought of them was a good thing for Sam Evans and his family.

In managing the bleachworks he was succeeded by a man of the name of Townsend, and at his death by his son Thomas. He was cut off suddenly in his youth and succeeded by John Wilcock, junior, a branch of the old Wilcock family. Ezekiel Grayson, senior, took the place, and afterwards was followed by Joseph Bibby. The late William Sanderson was employed at the works for fifty years, thirty of which he was manager. From his young manhood he was connected with the Wesleyans, and for a long course of years as an official he did much useful work in the Society, and specially as a local preacher. The collapsing of the aforementioned industries have greatly lessened the number of the mill hands. As to weavers and hacklers they have entirely disappeared, and as to bleachers the number has dwindled down to less than half-a-dozen. Twenty or thirty years ago there were seven hundred hands or more at the two mills - High and Low Bentham, and now there is about one hundred and fifty employed at the high mill.

Inns and Beerhouses

Amongst the lesser industries which have gone down the following may be mentioned: The old Kings Arms, once the head inn, is now a large grocery and general provision establishment. The Victoria Inn, near the station, has been made into the vicarage to St. Margarets. Mr. Seed's house was the Black Horse beerhouse. The new workhouse, which was a beerhouse, is now a grocers shop. There was a beerhouse in a house a little on the west of Mr. Holmes' druggist shop. There was a beerhouse in a house a little on the west side of Linga Cross, the name of the place is called Tennant House. The malt kiln at Moons Acre, as well as the one at Guy Hill, built by Mr. Burrow, was intimately connected with the liquor trade at Bentham. It may be concluded they have gone down.

Mr. William Burrow the elder added that of spirit dealer to his ordinary trade. In course of years Mr. John Titterington, of Moons Acre, for some reason added to his trade of maltmaking that of dealing in ardent spirits. Mr. Burrow could not bear the thought of a rival to poach on his grounds, and to compensate himself for any loss he built a large malt kiln which was carried on for many years. The trade in malt and spirits at Guy Hill and Moons Acre declined and was banished years ago. The late Mr. William Titterington, of Bentham, after he retired from the Horse and Farrier Inn opened a spirit vault at the east portion of the village, which, no doubt, collapsed after his death. It may be said to the credit of the deceased gentleman that he had so much regard for the sacredness of the Lords Day that when he was at the Horse and Farrier Inn he closed it all day on Sunday. Where his reverence, the priest, lives in Robbin-lane was at one time a beerhouse.

Nailmaking and Carrying

The nail making trade was of only small dimensions, and not many men were employed in it. My impression is that after Mr. Blackburn gave up the business and went to America it was carried on for some time by a young man of the name of Wilman from Wray, who served his apprenticeship with Mr. Blackburn. The carrying trade for a small village like Bentham at one time was rather important. Old John Sedgwick and Son did a large business between Bentham, Lancaster, and Settle. Roger Carr and brothers of Lowther Hill, kept wagons, carts, and many horses to carry finished goods to Lancaster and to bring back flax, hemp, and other materials for the Mill Company. Old John Phipps kept regularly four horses and carts going to Ingleton Colliery for coals for the mill. Old Tommy Camm, who when I saw him walked on two sticks and lived at Seat Hall, kept three horses and carts with a driver going daily for Ingleton coal for the bleaching works. Tommy from his age was feeble, still he could manage to hobble with his sticks to Bentham Mill once a quarter for his pay. On one occasion when with his money in his pocket he was toddling up that long lane on the west of Moons Acre to his home, he was stopped by a highwayman who demanded his money. As the old man was too feeble to make any resistance he had to give up his hard earned money. There was no doubt as to the man being a Benthamer, but it was in the dusk of the evening and the old man could not recognise him.

New Industries

None of them are of very large dimensions, same as a Mill Company, &c., still they show that the tradesmen and tradeswomen of High Bentham know how to push their craft. Some of them who are more energetic and spirited than their contemporaries have made good headway, but it is likely they would not wish it to be named how they by thrift and uprightness in trade transactions have risen from small beginnings. The "*self help*" tradesmen, the Co-operatives, by good management and united effort have founded a sound and successful business on their compact premises in the Station Road. Between sixty and seventy years ago a Co-operative Society was formed, and they began business in the shop now occupied by Wilcock and Sons. The design of their sign was two hands locked in each other under which was the motto, "*United we stand, divided we fall.*" I believe the society was largely supported by the bleachers.

Mr. James Procter's corn, &c., industry is now on a different plan altogether to what it was in the time of Hornby and Co. The old spinning machinery has been taken out and machinery of a much stronger make put in. The company is now drafted into a syndicate and assumes the name of "the Bentham Hemp Spinning Company." The work done by the new class of machinery is chiefly tube and belt weaving and spinning yarn for twine. In referring back it may be said that John Constantine was the general manager under the original company, that is when the affair was a private concern. Afterwards it was formed into "the Bentham Mill Co.", when Miles Constantine was the general manager. His successor was Ezekiel Grayson, who was after a few years management removed to Manchester to represent the company. The post was then taken by Mr. A. G. Cliborn, who still has the general management of the concern. It may be stated that it is to his skilful management that the mill has been able to run as usual during the coal famine with the exception of one or two days. It has been greatly to the benefit of the mills to keep them so fully employed.

T. MARSHALL,
COMPLETE HOUSE FURNISHER,
AND BEDDING WAREHOUSEMAN,
BENTHAM.
Plain and Artistic Furniture made to any design.
Carpets, Linoleums, Oilcloths, etc

MARSHALL'S, BENTHAM

No.8 (30th December, 1893)

The Social Condition of Bentham Sixty Years Ago

Social or socialism - companion or companionship - is now a very difficult thing to define, for as used in the press, novels, and by extreme revolutionisers it may mean Owenism, Communism, Keir Hardyism, or some other ostracism - a king of levelling down and robbing the thrifty and industrious to enrich the idle and thriftless. Happily such wild notice of using the fruits of other mens labour, either by violence or division, did not prevent the people of Bentham from pursuing their various avocations with honest intentions. As a small community they mutually agreed to live peaceably, and when needful to help one another. Though there was this kind of village brotherhood each family had its own dwelling or home, and many of the inhabitants endeavoured to lead a quiet and peaceable life in all godliness and honesty (St. Paul).

It could not be said that there were any rich people in the village, though some were in better circumstances than others. The inhabitants were chiefly tradesmen, farmers, mill hands, &c. There were a few old men who were too feeble to follow any employment, and there were not half-a-dozen who lived on their means. Domestic servants were very little needed, as most of the women did their own household work. A charwoman or a small girl might be employed a half-day or a day occasionally. If the north side of old Bentham be taken at the farm house on the west end the farmer, who was a widower, and his son kept a housekeeper of the name of Ellershaw. From this farm house to the extreme end on the east I only remember one shop, and it was the grocers shop now occupied by Mr. Holmes, where a domestic was kept. The shopkeeper was the late James Burton, and the servants name was Margaret Harrison. There might be one at the Brown Cow Inn, kept by a landlord of the name of Perkin, but at this date I cannot bring it to my recollection.

On the south side of Bentham there was not a single domestic kept, with the exception of the Kings Arms, Black Bull, and Royal Oak. Even at the Royal Oak I only remember the landlady's niece, Mary Easterby, being there, excepting when brewing, &c., was going on. Certainly at fairs extra help was needed. My reason for writing this is to show what a homely people the old Benthamers were. They were plain in their manners and appearance, and they gave one another their Christian names, as Mary, Moll, Molly, or Mally, John, Jack, or Jackey, &c. There was no grumbling because one person was better off than his neighbour. The doctrine that private property and capital should be divided, that the idle and profligate might have a share of the plunder, was not advocated. If any one man or woman set herself up above her equals it was called poverty pride. As to servants it may be said they were kept at Grovehill, Bentham House, and at Mr. Overends at the Mill, but these places were outside old Bentham.

Wage Rates and Food Costs

Though wages of every description were on a low scale to what they are now, and provisions of many kinds much dearer, still there was comparatively little poverty. I knew all the poorest people and I cannot remember one case of extreme poverty. Children were decently but plainly clothed, and chiefly shod with good strong ringed clogs on weekdays. Twice a day they were fed on oatmeal porridge and hard riddlebread. This was their food for breakfast and supper. There were families who could not afford much flesh meat, who frequently had oatmeal porridge for dinner. This was done by honest people who preferred self-denial to getting into debt. Children were not brought up so much on coffee and tea as they are now, and as to wheaten-bread it was a treat to have it served to them at tea on Sunday afternoons. There was not much tea, sugar, &c., for children when tea was 6s. and 7s. a pound, raw sugar 6d., and lump sugar 9d. and 10d. a pound, and fine flour 40s. a pack.

In spite of this most of the families provided dainty dishes for Christmastide. Mothers, how ever limited might be their means, were sure to make the greatest feast in the year a merry day for the children. In the morning the children were up betimes going from door to door, especially to the shops, calling out with merry voices, "*Get up old wives and bake your pies, for it is Christmas day in the morning*". At that day it was usual for shopkeepers to give Christmas boxes to the children. The inhabitants in spite of low wages and long hours of labour managed by carefulness to live very comfortably. Though as a youth I never made enquiries about wages, still hearing other persons talk about them they are still fresh in my memory. A master mason of the name of Redmayne, who lived at Low Bentham, acted as a foreman in building two rows of cottages on the west of the high mill yard, and it was said that he had 16s. a week, and that each cottage complete cost £50 each. Two men called datal, or day men, worked on a farm connected with the mill at 11s. a week. Children when they first went to the mill had 1s. 6d. a week and young women 5s. 6d., joiners, bleachers, and other millhands, would not average 20s. a week. Flax dressers and weavers were paid by the hundredweight and the web or piece. These varied in price, according to the quality of the work done. Many families would have been badly off if it had not been for the small pittances earned by their children at the mill. Some wives had to use their wits to make "*ends meet*". There is much talk and discussion now as to what is a living wage, but little said about how the wives should use their husbands wages. In my youth there were wives who would have thought themselves well off if their income had been from 16s. to 18s. per week. There were women who kept their homes more comfortable on 16s. a week than others on 20. A wife that is well up in knitting, sewing, darning, tacking, and mending does much to lessen domestic expenses. I remember a bleacher's wife in Duke-street of the name of Holmes who had a fair number of little children, whom she clothed with much neatness especially on Sundays, which made some of her neighbours say, "*I wonder how she does it on 16s. a week; she mun pinch their bellies to cover their backs.*" Young men who are seeking wives should remember that one fourth of a living wage is in the careful management of a thoughtful wife.

Though the hours of labour were long the village boys and girls were full of life and fun when they had finished their days work. Their hours of labour were from 6 a.m. to 7 p.m., from Monday to Saturday. John Wilcock and Anthony Nicholson, who were employed in the joiners shop, one as a carpenter and the other as a turner in iron, used to work from 4 a.m. to 9 p.m., excepting on Saturday nights. Their extra hours of labour were soldering flies for the spinning frames. It appeared that this was a necessary work required to be done while the mill was at rest. Both of them were healthy men, and lived to a good old age.

The mill workers of sixty or seventy years ago would have rejoiced if the hours of labour had been curtailed in their day to their present limit. The Saturday half-holiday would have made the lads and lassies hurrah for the boon. At this time all the millhands appeared to be contented with their condition, for when there were trades union turn-outs for increased wages in Scotland, and England, and incendiarism, plunder, maiming, and even murder terrorising law abiding people in Scotland and England, the village was unmoved.

The Arrival of the Union

About 1833 a deputation was sent from the flax-dressers trades union, Leeds, to form a branch at Bentham, and as at that time such a combination was illegal great secrecy had to be observed. Two young men who were just out of their apprenticeship were persuaded to join the union, and they had to be smuggled into a small upper room on the left hand side of the back entrance to the Black Bull. The initiatory service was carried out in the following manner. The candidates were blindfolded while in a standing posture, when the master of the ceremony read Psalm 69 after which an awful oath of secrecy was administered. Before the uncovering of the eyes took place the members made a clattering noise with their feet to make the sight of a full sized painted human skeleton more impressive. No doubt the scenic daub was intended to seal the lips of the new members. However they were so shocked with the ceremony that they shortly afterwards withdrew from a union which was contrary to their profession as Christians. Shortly after the formation of the Union the Leeds friends sent another deputation to the Bentham flax-dressers to promote a strike for an increase of wages. After reasoning with the members on the matter, and pointing out how far their wages were below the scale of wages at Leeds, he found with much dissatisfaction that his arguments were in vain, as the men said, with their limited number of members, a turnout would be a failure. Shortly after this interview the Bentham Union collapsed and nothing more was heard of turn-outs.

Though so much had been said in favour of the social condition of old Bentham, and of the honesty and thrift of the majority of the inhabitants, it would be misleading to conclude that there were no "*black sheep*" amongst them, but as this matter relates to another subject it may be passed over in this paper.

The Political Condition of Bentham

The political state of Bentham was in such a condition that little can be said about it. There were no political meetings held, only on the pavement a little to the east of the Brown Cow Inn. It was here where Lord Morphet and Lord Milton used to address the public; as for electors there were but few in the village. On these occasions there was very little excitement, as the people concluded that it would make little difference to them which side should win. An old man who had been a Whig was persuaded to vote Tory, and when I asked him his reason he said, "*It'll never mak' a penny difference to us which side gits in*". There was a deal of this kind of politics then, and even now there are voters who have not advanced much in this respect. Of the few voters in the village they were almost to a man Tories. Mr. Roughsedge, who had great influence, was a Tory, and Mr. Overend, the general manager of the Mill Company, was a Tory, and as there were only about three voters amongst the mill hands, P. Wilson, J. Thornton, and R. Carr, they felt it would not do to vote against Mr. Roughsedge and the parson.

A laughable affair took place after an election between 40 and 50 years ago in the street on the west of the Methodist Chapel. The whole village was excited and a procession of Tories headed by the village band paraded the streets of Higher and Lower Bentham on their way to the Rectory. After manoeuvring for some time on the Rectory grounds and being well supplied with drink from the Rev. Mr. Robinsons cellar in token of their victory they started on their homeward journey to headquarters. Happening to be over at Bentham when the procession with flying banners came up the street I saw my father carrying the main colour and as I could see that he and others were under the potent influence of the parsons drink, I decided to wrench the flag from his hands, not with any intent to injure it. As the procession drew near, some of the Tories were suspicious of my intention of taking the flag. As the late Henry Langstreth approached me I let him take the flag and I seized my father in my arms and carried him, in spite of himself, into his house where he made no resistance. The reason why I did it was that so many of them were either drunk or sharp fresh that I did not like to see my father take such a prominent part in a drunken procession. There was of course much amusement, but no bad feeling was evoked, and the triumphing party marched on to the Cross where more drink could be had.

This excitement only lasted a few days when the village lapsed into its wanted political apathy. When the Chartists were getting up petitions in all the large towns in England and Scotland and terrorising by plunder and in some instances murder there was no political agitator at Bentham bold enough to enlighten the working men on the six points of the Charter which was to confer such wonderful benefits upon the working classes. The state of things today is wonderfully changed.

The Religious Condition of Bentham

Before 1820 there were neither church, chapel, nor Friends Meeting-house at High Bentham. The Methodists were a small body who met occasionally in the Kings Arms dancing-room on Sunday afternoons and in cottages on week nights. Of Church people at this time, there was a goodly number of them who attended Low Bentham Church. It was a long way to go from Mewith Head Hall, Mewith Head, and the neighbourhood. People at that time must have been of more hardy condition than they are now, for few men in the coldest and roughest weather when they went to church wore top coats. It would have been a rare sight if a boy had had a top coat on, and yet there was no fire in the church from the beginning of the year to its close. Though this was the case, and the service nearly a half-hour longer than Church services of the present day, there was less complaining of cold than there is when stoves are used.

In 1820 the Wesleyan Chapel was opened, shortly after which a Sunday school was started and carried on by mill hands. For some reason this school collapsed for a time, when a Church Sunday School was opened in the upper Grammar School on the monitor system, and superintended by John Maudsley, late of Clapham. Miss Parker, of Bentham House, and her governess companion, held a Sunday school for mill girls and others. Some time after Charles Parker and family left Bentham, the Friends dwindled down to two, Mary Townson and Mrs. Bellman. With the Low Bentham Friends, of which there were very few, they met for worship on Sunday mornings at Calfe Cop Meeting House. The Independents of High-street Chapel, Lancaster, occasionally held afternoon services at Bentham, but failed to form a church. Edward Bowker, a weaver at Kirkham, for a time opened his house for Nonconformist worship, but it was of short duration.

The political and religious condition of Bentham at the present day is far in advance of the past. An ancient custom in connection with the Sunday morning service at the Parish Church may be mentioned. At the close of the service, William Bond, the Clerk, went direct to the churchyard, and stood on a tomb opposite the southern door, to announce sales, &c., which would take place during that or next week. In September it was usual to call the neighbouring nut woods, and to state the punishment which would be inflicted on trespassers after nuts.

No.9 (6th January, 1894)

The Drinking Customs of Olden Times

Sixty or seventy years ago there was considerable drinking both by some of the working men and outside farmers. This was specially the case on market days, and at the two leading annual fairs. Some of the weavers, bleachers, and flaxdressers frequently went on the spree. A few tradesmen did too much at what was locally known as *"running the dobbiners"*, which was running at short intervals to the Inns for a glass of ale, &c., and then back to their business. This daily habit was considered more expensive than an occasional spree. The flaxdressers were paid monthly, but some of them who could not get a month's provisions on credit were paid in part at the end of the fortnight. This was called *"kicking"*. It was a regular thing for some of the men to do without drink for three weeks or more before going on the spree again for a day or two, and sometimes a week. One man who was not a regular drinker, when he did go on the spree, he loved the taste of ale so much that he drank it to excess so that he could not lift his glass to his mouth. It may not be believed, but still it is a fact that on one occasion when he was in this state he asked a pot companion to lift his glass to his mouth, but he refused, seeing that drink was running from his lips. One of the hecklers on one occasion when on the spree, for being in company with an itinerant sweep, he was discharged. The offensive was unintentionally given, and the rash act on the part of the late Mr. Overend, the general manager of the mills, was countermanded. The cause of it was, during a recent night some burglar or burglars had entered the mill yard, and by the use of a ladder had ascended the roof of the counting-house, stripped off some slates, and entered the upper offices, and committed a robbery. This discovery was so startling that Richard (Dick) Hoggarth, of Lancaster, was sent for at once. Though Mr. Hoggarth was very popular as a detective constable, he failed in this instance. The night watchman, an old man of the name of Tempest, could not account for his not hearing the burglars.

There was a good deal of oats grown in my youth, and much of it was sold by auction, and at such times the people who attended were well supplied with drink. At such sales some men were so besotted with drink that they bid when they were lying helplessly drunk on their backs. Drinks exercised opposite effects on the temperaments of the drinkers, so that one of the leading shoemakers, when he was fuddled, smiled all the face over, and could say nothing worse than, *"Joys, thou knows, and let us be merry and peaceable."* Another tradesman, on whom it had a different effect, stamped, shouted, and used the most offensive language. Windows were smashed, glasses broken, and doors kicked, and all this was done without the interference of a parish constable.

The special occasions for intemperate drinking were Christmas and the two fairs at Easter and the 22nd and 23rd of June. For these principal holidays of the year the Innkeepers made special brewings, in addition to which many villagers and outside farmers did the same at home for Christmas. There were many men who indulged a little in John Barleycorn on those holiday seasons who, during the other portions of the year were strictly sober. Much good ale of a better tap was considered necessary to make Christmas a season of joyous mirth. The Church singers at Christmas were not proof against the many temptations that beset them to drink, and as the farmers in Mewith, Tatham, and other places had their Christmas taps, the singers were well supplied with home brewed. As the winters were much severer sixty and seventy years ago than they are now, strange incidents often took place before the singers reached their homes. Occasionally the bum fiddle and other instruments were lost in the snowdrifts, and those men who had drunk the deepest either lagged behind or lost their way. Often when they did arrive at Bentham their thirst for drink was so far from being assuaged that they went to one of the public-houses to continue their carousal until midnight. This was at a time when public inns were open from the first of January to the thirty-first of December.

One Christmas day, at night, between fifty and sixty years ago, I went into the Royal Oak to seek a friend to advise him to go home, when the village blacksmith accosted me with the words, *"Are you pious?"* I could not but feel sorry for him, for he had been a reformed drunkard, and, to the joy of his friends, had taken to teaching in the Church Sunday School. In my further search I went into a small parlour on the right hand side where the Church singers were all seated and singing at the top of their voices with their eyes shut and their bodies and heads swaying backwards and forwards. In the company were some of the leading men in the village, and they were all too drunk to take notice of my presence. After looking at them with pity I turned away thankful that I was a total abstainer. The Church singers were only on a par with the choirs of other townships, and, as a rule, the public looked upon such things at Christmas with complacency, observing it was Christmas time, and it was well to enjoy themselves.

The Easter Fair

The throngest cattle fair in the year was that which took place on Easter Saturday, and when it reached its utmost popularity as a cattle fair Good Friday had to be utilised for a market. On this day the parish banks and other fields were white with cattle, and, according to an old custom, boys, girls, and men led the poor cows a weary toil by running them to the ditches and corners of the fields to milk them. If the weather was favourable this milking continued until the cattle were driven into the fair the next morning. This was a special occasion for the villagers laying in a good stock of rich new milk, cream, and in some instances butter. The number of cattle dealers, &c., was so large at the Easter fairs that the innkeepers were in the habit, previous to their taking place, of engaging all the spare beds obtainable in the village for Good Friday night. Men used to all the comforts of home life were glad to get into any kind of a clean bed, even in rooms open to the roof in which there were three beds occupied. Cattle drovers and others had to take the stables, haylofts, or any nook and corner where they might find shelter. In the evening of Good Friday all the inns were crowded, and every available room was filled with men, smoking, drinking, bargaining, and disputing about cattle and other things. I have a vivid impression of a scene of this character which took place in a parlour at the Brown Cow over 70 years ago.

Though there were four public houses so near to each other that a man used to drinking might have drunk a glass of ale in each in less than a quarter of an hour, the landlord of the Black Bull fixed a drinking booth on the open space at the other side of the street to his house. On Easter Sunday evening there was a good deal of moderate drinking by villagers who did not frequent public houses at any other time of the year. It was the day for drinking mulled ale, and many religious persons did not think there was any wrong in visiting one of the inns, and in an upper room smoke their pipes and sip a glass or two of the luscious beverage. Even pious women did not consider there was any inconsistency in sitting with their husbands for the same purpose. I can vouch for their consistent lives in other matters, and the reason for stating this Easter Sunday affair is to show what a hold the ancient custom of drinking mulled ale on that day had on the general public. It was before teetotalism had made its way to Bentham.

The June Fair

Though there was a good deal of drinking at the June Fair, it was confined chiefly to the holiday keepers in the neighbourhood, as the cattle market was on a very limited scale. The second day was the greatest event of the year for young folks who came to witness the procession of the Samaritan Sick Club. The flag, which represented the scene in the Gospel, and the Club sticks, were kept in a large room at the north end of Bentham House. One of the Club sticks, which had yellow knobs or heads, was doled out to each member to walk with in the procession to and from the Parish Church at Low Bentham. Some of the members showed a little pride of their position on the march, especially if they had had a little quantity of drink before the start. Many of the members, on reaching the Punch Bowl Inn, at a short distance on the east of the Church, preferred staying there to listening to a sermon on brotherly love and the benefits of sick societies to working men. My attention was much taken by an official who was under the influence of drink, and who made strenuous efforts in the march to steady himself in vain. He was one of those men who felt his chains, and often tried to break them, but in vain. Shortly after this date he was induced to attend the Primitive Methodists meeting at Low Bentham, and eventually he became a member, and then a zealous and consistent local preacher. On his removal to Lancaster he made his influences for good felt amongst the Primitives there. He occasionally visited the two Benthams, and at such times he preached in the open air in the space of ground on the west side of the old poorhouse at High Bentham, when, with his clear and ringing voice, he told the people what Christianity had done for him - a poor miserable slave to drink and the Devil. Had he been living, no man could have given a more solid testimony that he that Christianity was not played out. I believe some of his descendants are still about Lancaster, and walking in the steps of their father. There is no need to suppress his name, as his reformed life was honourably and usefully spent in the service of his Divine Master, and his name (William Benn) is gratefully remembered in many of the homes of the Primitives at Lancaster, Skerton, and the neighbourhood.

Duck Hunts

The day after the fair was an idle day with some of the village workmen and tradesmen, and as they all met in one or more of the public inns, they were sure of concocting some plan to keep up the excitement in the village. For the afternoon amusement a duck hunt on the mill dam, in the river Wenning, near Bentham House was planned. Dogs and ducks were provided for the amusement, which was much enjoyed by a crowd of spectators, who had little feeling for dumb animals. It was evidently a pleasure to them to see the ducks swimming at their utmost speed to escape their pursuers and then, when hotly pursued, diving to make their escape. When the ducks remained a considerable time under the surface the discussion was as to where they would rise. Happily this form of cruelty was discontinued before many of the present generation were born. The evening amusement was chairing the Mayor. At times it was a rather difficult thing to obtain a suitable man to act the part of Mayor. When this was the case drink was freely supplied to some loafer to get himself to be made a fool and a laughing stock to a gaping crowd. The Mayors were generally drunk when they were put in a chair and hoisted upon the shoulders of four carriers. As a rule they were ignorant men and not well adapted for making short bright speeches. Sometimes a man of more than ordinary education and wit volunteered his services when he was sure to give the publicans and tradespeople some good hits which would please the listening crowds, and evoke hurrahs and "*Weel done Mayor, pitch into them, give them another good rub, for some of them deserve it.*" The following are a few specimens.

Chairing Mayors

In the procession the Mayor was generally taken to the fronts of the public houses, when it was evident from the manner of the Mayor, who was not so drunk as he pretended, that he was not going to mince matters. In a loud and clear voice he demanded an interview with the landlord and landlady saying, "*As I have been elected to the honourable position of Mayor of the loyal and ancient town of Bentham, I have thought it my first duty to come and direct you how to deal with the subjects of my Sovereign Master King George the fourth.*" Then he told them to brew good ale, made of genuine malt and hops and not to water their liquors, but to let their customers have them of a proper degree of strength. They were to allow no drunkenness and brawling and fighting in their houses, and to mind and keep good order, and to close their door at a reasonable hour, as it was wrong to keep working men and others from their homes to untimely hours. Those remarks pleased the crowd who shouted, "*Well done Mayor, you have given some sound advice.*" At the grocers he would say, "*I have heard that some of you moisten your tobacco, put a little sand in your sugar, alum in your flour, and that your tea and coffee are adulterated. To do such things cannot be allowed, as the health of the inhabitants would not only be injured but they would to some extent be robbed as really as if a highwayman had picked their pockets.*" For the present the Mayor said he would condone the offence, but if in the future such offences were repeated he would inflict severe punishment on the wrong doers. To the farmers he said he was sorry to be informed that some of them were not as fair traders as the laws and customs of the honourable borough required them to be. He understood that some of them watered their milk, and as to their wives and daughters they did not work their butter as they should do, consequently butter milk was left in so that it failed to keep sweet. There was much cheering at such plain and well directed hits at such malpractices. It was only now and then that a Mayor of this character was obtainable, but when it was so there was a good deal of harmless fun and the people enjoyed it. It is likely that there are few persons living in Bentham who remember the ancient custom of chairing mayors.

Drunken Fights

Such excessive drinking generally resulted in brawls and fighting. Certainly much of the fighting at the fairs was caused by outsiders. In the four villages Burton-in-Lonsdale, Ingleton, Clapham, and Bentham there were men who went to the local fairs for a spree and quarrel and a good fight. At Bentham these fair brawls were sure to end in two or three or more battles, which chiefly took place in a small croft behind the Kings Arms. At these conflicts the croft was crowded so that the combatants had scarcely room to pommel one another to their hearts content. By their backers, each side was well supported, and while the battle was moving from place to place the crowd had to give way that the men might have breathing room. The shouting at times was almost deafening, one shouting, *"Weel done Charlie, or weel done Bob, hit him hard."* The trees on the east side were crowded with big boys as there was no other way of seeing the battle. When the fight was over the shouting on the winning side was tremendous. The victor was patted on the back and flattered with such words as *"Charlie thous licked him weel this time, itll be a long time before hell craw oor thee again."* This flattery made the victors think that they had done some brave deed. In my young days men could fight as often as they liked, and as long as they liked without the interference of the parish constable. This freedom to quarrel and fight lasted almost up to the time when Mr. Exton was stationed first at Burton-in-Lonsdale, and then removed to Ingleton.

In my time I have frequently acted in brawls and fights as a voluntary policeman. Over forty years ago, when residing at Kirkby Lonsdale, I went over to one of the Bentham fairs. As I entered the village on the west the first thing that took my attention was four men fighting in the street in front of the Horse and Farrier Inn. I went at once to the two nearest and rushed between them and stopped the fight, and then acted in the same way with the other two combatants. It was amusing to hear some of the lookers on say, *"Whea is 'e."* I had not been long in my fathers before I heard a cry in the street, *"Theres a battle."* This was in the street before the Black Horse beerhouse, the house now occupied by Mr. Seed, cabinet maker, acting the part of a constable I parted them at once. In all my experience in this work I never met with any difficulty in stopping a fight if there was not a crowd around it. Though I have had some rough experiences and have had my face and coat stained with blood, I was never struck between the combatants though on some occasions they struck at each other round my neck. I do not think the men I parted in the street were Bentham men, and as they were out of the fair, which was always confined to the other end of the village, there were very few persons looking on. The history of the temperance movement in the next article will be a pleasant contrast with the present one.

> DID YOU KNOW THAT YOU CAN BUY FURNITURE, AMERICAN ORGANS, AND HARMONIUMS, BENTHAM MADE,
> AT J. W. SEED'S.
> "What?" "Made at Bentham!" "Yes!"
> DEALER IN PIANOS. &c. REPAIRS MOST REASONABLE. GOOD VALUE GIVEN AT
> SEED'S, BENTHAM. ENQUIRY SOLICITED. [129

No.10 (13th January, 1894)

The Introduction of the Temperance Movement

In speaking of the introduction of total abstinence into Bentham, the writer must necessarily speak of himself as he was the first pledged total abstainer in the district. Somewhere about 1833, a Preston temperance advocate fell into my hands, when, after becoming acquainted with its teachings, I mentally pledged myself a total abstainer from all intoxicating drinks. At that time I was an occasional drinker of small beer which the village publicans sold at one penny a quart. A mental pledge was only practicable, as there was no temperance society in the country, unless there was one at Lancaster. As all the men, young and old, drank more or less of ale and spirits, it may be concluded that my abstinence was more noticeable on that account. I made it a subject of conversational discussion, I met with no persecution on that account. I may be excused, though it looks like boasting, when I say that total abstinence has been worth more to me in body, mind, circumstances, and home life than untold gold. Where are the young men of my youth, some of whom were many years younger than myself? They are all gone! gone! twenty or more years, and some of them were slaves to the alcoholic drinks. On my removal to Lancaster in the spring of 1835, I joined the Temperance Society at the old Sugar House, and during my stay in the ancient borough, with other young men I spoke at temperance meetings, all of whom are likely dead with the exception of Mr. Samuel Bond.

At the end of two years I returned to Bentham, when I began to hold teetotal meetings in the open air, as schools and chapels were closed against teetotalism as an ungodly and unnatural thing. At that time there was no one to help in speaking, though there was no backwardness in attending meetings, and joining in the singing. Some idea may be formed how the new doctrine was viewed by some of the drinkers and the respectable inhabitants. At this early period of the cause, when speaking in the open air, an old pensioner (Tom Heaton) was so grieved that he went to my home to make a complaint, saying that I was a disgrace to the family preaching such stuff as teetotalism, for how could people live without good ale.

Views on Tee Totalism

The following instance will show how respectable people looked upon teetotalism. One evening when holding a meeting near the entrance to the square, Mr. Edward Overend, eldest son of Mr. Overend, head manager of the mills, happened to pass when I was holding an open air meeting; shortly after, meeting with my sister he said, "*Your brother is a fool to talk such nonsense as teetotalism*". On another occasion when holding an open air meeting opposite the Black Bull, Charnley, the landlord, got so excited that he brought a number of glasses of ale and put them on the front of a cart which was standing at the door, for any of the people to drink. He then went to his house and returned with a bottle of ginger-beer, rushed across the street and handed it to me. At another meeting two young men, one of whom was Charlie Lupton, stood one on each side of the chair to draw off my attention that they might pull the chair from under me. Another occasion the landlord of the Brown Cow interrupted the meeting.

Coming to later times, at one of the fairs I held a meeting on the old Kings Arms front when seeing the late Frank Twistleton in the crowd I asked him to speak. Afterwards when I was speaking a stranger came up and interrupted the meeting. Amongst the provoking words he used, he called out, "*You and your wife have just come out of Bellevue Prison,*" - a place we had never seen. In the afternoon a good meeting was held near the entrance to the square. The same opponent, who was said to be a brewer, came again and repeated the same charge. I asked him to be quiet until I had done speaking then he might take the chair and have his say. Mrs. John Braithwaite, who had lent the chair called out, "*Nay, he shan't hev my chair*". There was a rather amusing instance at this meeting. A tall military-looking man, with a cap on his head, and under the influence of drink, came into the crowd. I mentioned an instance in which a man had been treated by his "*pot*" companions when he was in a drunken sleep, which was that of having his face blacked and the hair of his head cut short. He took this as an offence and lifting his cap called out, "*Do you mean me?*" It was afterwards said that he had had his hair cut in a similar way. Though I told him that I did not mean him he challenged me to fight. I said wait until I have done speaking and I will fight you. He afterwards calmed down and became quite attentive and when the brewer came again to interrupt the meeting, he went into the fair to seek a policeman. In the summer of 1842 I attended an open air service on the open space on the west of the old poorhouse, when the late Mr. Child, so popular at Leeds in connection with the Rifle Engineers, occupied the chair, and I and the Rev. Thomas Savage, superintendent of the Settle Circuit, spoke at the meeting. Mr. Child at the time was a mechanic at the high mill. Shortly after the meeting Mr. Savage and I were fellow travellers to London, he to the Wesleyan Conference, and I forward to the Continent.

Mr. Thomas Leeming, who in his early life lived many years at Bentham, did good service in the temperance cause. In 1835 or 1836, Messrs. H. Snell, J. Harger, and other friends from Settle, visited Bentham twice, and on both occasions for want of a room held their meetings on the School Hill. After this meeting it appears Mr. Leeming went to a meeting in the Kings Arms dancing room, where he offered to sign the temperance pledge, but was objected to because his father kept a beer-house, and he himself was taking lessons in the art of brewing at the Brown Cow Inn. He remembers being at the meeting already referred to on the ground near the old workhouse. Mr. Leeming signed the temperance pledge on Whit Monday in 1840. When the L. N. Western Railway was in course of construction, Mr. Leeming called upon Mr. Thomas Geldard, acting trustee of the Wesleyan Chapel, to ask the loan of it for a public meeting and temperance tea party. He consented on one condition and that was that the temperance party would never make a similar request. The public tea was under the management of Mr. Leeming and Mr. C. Knowles. Evidently this was the first temperance tea party held at Bentham. In the years between 1843 and 1850, Mrs. Jackson, a popular temperance lecturer, visited Bentham. Mr. T. B. Thompson, of Leeds, Mr. Crawford, and others came to Bentham on the same mission. After the Wesleyan Conference withdrew its opposition to the temperance movement, the Chapel was opened for meetings.

Mr. C. Knowles says he came to live at Bentham either in 1841 or 1842, and he remembers two Preston friends visiting the village on a temperance mission. For want of a room they held their meeting on the opposite side of the street to the house in which Mr. Leeming lives. This would be on the School Hill. Mr. Knowles signed the pledge of total abstinence at Settle in 1835. Some time after settling at Bentham he did much to promote temperance principles by opening his shop for supplying tea, coffee, and other refreshments to the public at the house and shop now occupied by Mr. Seed, cabinet maker. After taking possession of the Kings Arms under the late Mr. Rice, he extended his grocery business as well as pushing on more vigorously temperance refreshments. Much business was done in this way on market days, but especially at the annual fairs. Mr. Rice stands out prominently as a philanthropist and a warm friend of the temperance movement, or he would not have bought the property of the late landlord, Mr. Atkinson, so that one of the ancient public inns of the village might be closed for the sale of articles of alcoholic drinks and opened for the sale of articles of food, &c. Mr. Knowles continued the sale of refreshments to those who preferred his house to a public inn until the extension of his provision trade made it necessary to give it up. When penny reading came into vogue they were given in connection with the Band of Hope and temperance meetings. From this date Mr. Knowles took a warm interest in the temperance movement, which he has retained to the present date. About 1854 there was a revival of the cause, when the late Mr. Rice and others took an active part in it.

The Origins of the Band of Hope

The information of this event appears to be beyond the ken of the present Bentham temperance friends. I remember in the far past there was a Band of Hope and the meetings were held at the gate house at the entrance to the Mill yard. I did not live at Bentham at that date, but frequently went over, and on one occasion (if not more) I spoke at the meetings. The late Geo. Phillipson and other leading Methodists carried it on. The promoters of it long ago passed from their Christian labour. A boys fife band was formed, which was useful in making the meetings more attractive and of drawing larger numbers of boys and girls to their practice nights. On some festive occasions, I believe that of Christmas, the band went round the country, and at many places the lads were tempted and pressed to drink. Some of them yielded, which caused much strife and dissatisfaction, the result of which was the Fife Band collapsed and the Band of Hope was disbanded.

The Temperance Society for many years was carried on too much with fits and starts. Of the present societies more certain knowledge may be given. In 1889 the Wesleyan Band of Hope was formed, when the Rev. Mr. Jenkins was its first president, and Mr. R. Sanderson its conductor. Though under Conference rule, it is so far unsectarian that the children of any or no church are eligible for membership. The Rev. Mr. Jackson succeeded Mr. Jenkins on his removal to another circuit. The present president is the Rev. J. T. Marquand, the vice-president being Mr. Joseph Coulam. Mr. N. Saul, who was conductor up to his death, which took place a few weeks ago, was a long, faithful, and earnest worker in the movement. Secretary, C. Knowles; Treasurer, J. Coulam; Registrar, Miss Vickers. The meetings are held in the Wesleyan Schoolroom fortnightly in winter and in summer, monthly. The number of members is 150.

The High Bentham Temperance Society

The information on the state of this Society is very meagre. It was reorganised in 1872. William Coates is President; J. Knowles, Treasurer; J. Knowles, Junr., Secretary. The Committee, which consists of fifteen members have to arrange meetings and conduct the business of the Society. Meetings are held occasionally in the winter season.

Bentham Mutual Temperance Club

This Club at its beginning was named Howson and Dawsons Club. As Dawson is dead, it is now generally named Anthony Howsons Club. It was founded in 1870 by the two men named and Richd. Smith. In its formation Mr. Rice did much to advance its prosperity. For the first year and for many years in succession its annual supper was held at Mr. C. Knowles. Since its discontinuance there it has been held at Mr. Hird's Temperance Hotel.

This Mutual Temperance club, which has become one of the principal institutions in the village, numbers fifty members. Its principal rule is that each member pays sixpence per week, which at the end of the year is refunded, that is, if during that time each member has kept his pledge; if not, it is forfeited. By forfeits and bank interest the funds of the Club are augmented. As the forfeits and bank interest are at the disposal of the members they generously contribute to the funds of the Band of Hope.

Andrew Dawson, one of the founders of the Club, was a striking instance of what teetotalism can do in recuperating a wreck of a constitution and of adding some years to a life that hung in the balance. His reformation was a marvel to the whole village, and his recovery to health was rapid and his pleasures of life greatly increased. During many years of his abstinence he lived with Mrs. Turner at the Plough Inn, and it was very much to her credit that she always encouraged him to keep his pledge. Though it was a matter of regret to his friends that a short time before his death the old appetite revived and overcame him, still that does not reflect on teetotalism as a perfect cure of intemperance. Mr. H. Howson is president and secretary of the Club, and Mr. J. Coulam treasurer. The Mutual Temperance Club has done good service to its members and the village, and it is to be hoped that at the beginning of the New Year it will register a goodly number of new members.

The Religious Condition of Bentham

It has been already stated that in 1810 there was neither Church nor Chapel in Upper Bentham. The Wesleyan Chapel was built in 1820, and it was named Armenian Chapel on a stone tablet fixed in the wall above the doorway. The foundation of St. Margaret's, built by the late Mr. Roughsedge, was laid by Miss Roughsedge, June 30th, 1835. The Friends Meeting House was built in 1854. At the Methodist Sunday School there are 158 scholars and 25 teachers. There are also two superintendents, two secretaries, two librarians, and a treasurer. In the Church Sunday School there are 164 scholars and 10 teachers. The Friends have a schoolroom adjoining the Meeting House, but information as to whether it is a Sunday school is not to hand. The Friends number about 50 members, including Upper and Nether Benthams. In addition there are attendants who are not identified with the membership.

The Primitives have entirely disappeared from the two Benthams. About 1836 or 1837 the Rev. Mr. Langham, of the Settle Primitive Home Mission, visited Upper Bentham for the purpose of forming a branch society. He was a zealous and laborious home missionary, and he began his work by open air services. A young minister of the name of Jones joined him in the mission and did much good service to the cause at Bentham. He was an emotional preacher, and became so popular that Church people, Wesleyans, and those persons who seldom attended a place of worship flocked to his ministry. When the weather became too cold for open air services, preaching was conducted in cottages. They were held in a cottage at the north end of the Hall yard for a time, and then removed to Stephen Howards, where a society was formed. Afterwards for a considerable time meetings were held in cottages at Nether Bentham. At one time they were held in a room connected with the Royal Oak Inn. The society and congregations increased considerably, so that a new chapel was built just out of the village, on the west, to meet the convenience of the Primitives of the two villages. The chief leaders of the cause were Miss Davis, William Walker & Sons, Joshua Banks, Robert Shuttleworth, William Benn and his father-in-law, Mr. Smith, the village tailor. Eventually, through removals to Lancaster and Barnoldswick, near Colne, both the society and the congregation dwindled down so much that the chapel was closed as a place of worship and made into a commodious and comfortable house.

No.11 (20th January, 1894)

Stirring Events: High Bentham Mill Fire

One of the most exciting events of the past was the disastrous fire at the High Mill, May 19th, 1803, and though it was some years before my time, still it may be of some interest to the present inhabitants to read what was told me in my early days. The mill was singularly, but unintentionally, set on fire by John Phipps, the fireman. The fireman's work included that of looking after the engine. Through friction one of the wheels became red hot, and when it was discovered by the fireman he was so alarmed that he seized a bucket which appeared to be full of water and threw the contents on the wheel, when all at once the engine was enveloped in flames. Unfortunately the bucket was filled with oil. Though the alarm was given at once the fire spread so rapidly that shortly the mill itself was on fire.

The cry of fire spread from room to room which made the workers rush to the outlets to make their escape. It was not many minutes before the whole village was aroused, and men and women were running in every direction either to render help or with others to look at the burning fabric. Flax, yarn, and everything that could be handled was thrown through the windows or carried out from the low room into the mill yard so as to be out of the way of the fire.

Charles Parker, the acting partner of the company, was shortly amongst the people entreating them not to unnecessarily risk their lives as he would rather that all was burnt than one life should be lost. Though most of the machinery was destroyed, a large portion of flax and yarn was saved. The fire caused the utmost excitement through a wide district, and especially on the high banks of the Wenning. Groups of farmers and their families stood on the high ground where they could look down the valley at the fire, and even mothers carried their babies in their arms, and mixed up with the lookers on. The late Mr. Thomas Leeming, of Nook Dales, said that his mother, when he was a baby, carried him in her arms that she might see the fire. The day on which the fire took place was Holy Thursday, and on that day it was a custom for the mill joiners to take a days fishing with nets up the Dale Beck on the east side of Ingleton for the Lord of the Manor. The men saw the clouds of smoke which hung over the neighbourhood of Bentham, but they could not make out the cause of it. Charles Parker, who was a kind-hearted employer of labour, managed to find his hands some kind of work until the mill was put in order for work again.

Local Suicides

When I was a mere child an event took place which not only startled the whole neighbourhood, but caused a widespread feeling of sorrow for Tommy Newhouse and his wife Esther. They had a son, generally called young Tommy, who was a quiet and inoffensive man. Through some love affair, which he took very keenly to heart, life became a burden too heavy for him to bear. He lived with his father and mother in a small cottage on the west side of what is now King-street. At that time it was in the Kings Arms Yard, and it was the only cottage in it. One Sunday afternoon, when he had determined to put an end to his intolerable grief, he went to a house somewhere on the south side of the Wenning to borrow a gun, saying he had seen a hare. He afterwards went into a wood on the south side of Lane Foot and blew out his brains. My father, who with some other men went to convey his remains to his home. said that his brains were scattered in every direction, some of them were hanging on the branches of the trees.

The village was greatly excited, and the shock on his mother left her a maniac, and the feeling greatly deepened. She became so unmanageable that she had to be taken to an asylum, where by kind treatment in course of time she was considered sufficiently recovered to leave the asylum. After her restoration she lived many years at her old home.

Her late son in his trouble had selected a chapter - first in the Book of Lamentations - which he thought was descriptive of his sorrows, and for many years it was spoken of as Tommy Newhouses chapter. I and my sisters were generally asked to read a chapter in the Bible on a Sunday before retiring to bed, and I remember well how my father sometimes said, "*Read Tommy Newhouse's chapter*". I have reason to believe that the chapter was often read in other families in remembrance of Tommy Newhouse's sad end.

I remember two other cases of suicide in my early boyhood, but I will only mention one, which excited a good deal of sympathy. Though this happened when I was about eleven years of age, I have still a clear impression of the occurrence. Her name was Atkinson, and she was a respectable servant at Bentham House. Her trouble was through a young man of the name of Barker, and to end her grief she went out one dark night, climbed the parapet of the bridge, which at that time was lower than what it is now, and dropped into the mill dam. Her corpse was carried by some of the mill joiners to her home at Mooter Beck, a house on the south side of the Wenning. This was a case that evoked considerable public sympathy, for the family was much respected and connected with the Friends Meeting House at Calfe Cop.

An Accident - and a Hoax

A sad accident and a marvellous escape took place near the late Richard Green's, Green Smithy. Dorothy Balderston, landlady of the Hen and Chickens public house, Burton-in-Lonsdale, was coming home from a visit in Bowland, and being driven by an elderly man, whom she employed, when, some distance from the place where the driver was killed, the spirited horse took fright and started down the road, which was a steep descent of three-quarters of a mile, to Wenning Bridge, at a terrible speed, without being checked until it reached Bentham. The driver sat on the front of the cart, and when he fell off, the horse sent one of its shoe heels into his forehead. Mrs. Balderston's was a most wonderful escape, and how she managed to keep her place in the conveyance was a matter of astonishment. The accident occurred about 1831 or 1832.

A mean and cruel hoax practised upon two old folks of the names of Kitty and Molly Minikin caused much indignation and much kind sympathy to the old people. They had a son called Jimmy Minikin, a flax-dresser at Barnard Castle. One day a stranger called to see them, and after introducing himself as a man from the town mentioned, he said he had brought them sad news. He described their sons illness and death, and how he had been sent at once as a special messenger to inform them of the sad event, so as to give them time to attend his funeral. He then told them that it had made such a painful impression on his wife that she was unable to attend to any business, not even to be informed that he had been requested to take information to them. On this account he had been told to ask the old people to lay down money to pay his expenses. Not suspecting any fraud, they paid the money, and the hard hearted wretch left, no doubt chuckling at the success of his device. Paying the money was not the worst, for, as the old people wished to see their son before his funeral they hired a horse and cart, as no other conveyance was kept in the village, and set off for Barnard Castle, a distance of sixty or seventy miles. On their arrival they found that their son and his family were in good health. As a matter of course though deceived they were glad to see them.

A stirring and amusing affair took place one market day, the market at that time being on a Monday. The cause of it was the seizing of a black horse belonging to a man of the name of Berry. The lawyer who seized the horse was the late Mr. Ellethorne of Lancaster. The seizure took place near the Royal Oak, when there was, for a village, an immense crowd who were in sympathy with Mr. Berry. Mr. Ellethorne was very much excited, and threatened what he would do to those men who helped Berry to recover his horse. Maister Wildman, the second master of the Grammar School, was ordered to take down the names of those who jostled one another against the person who had charge of the horse. After considerable moving about in the crowd, Berry's friends recovered the horse, lifted him on it, when the crowd made him a passage, and he galloped at a quick speed up Robbin Lane. The shouting and hurrahing was tremendous, and the scene so exciting and vivid that after seventy years it is still in ones memory.

The annual Catherine Hunt was held in November in honour of Queen Catherine. The hounds belonged to the Rev. Mr. Wigglesworth, Town End, Slaidburn, and the huntsman was John Ayrton. A hare was always sent to Mr. Roughsedge, for which he gave a sovereign, which was handed to the huntsman. The flax dressers, who kept up the annual hunt, always took supper at one of the inns, which was generally the Black Bull. The women at the Mill celebrated the day with a public tea and a dance. Before the huntsman departed for home many of his friends used to see him off. Before the final parting took place, sometimes two or three bowls of punch were drunk at the public-house door. Some of the leading men of the village used to share in the carousal, when they would throw a shilling into the bowl or a half-crown, which meant more drink.

The Local Hunt

The following is a scene I witnessed at the Black Bull door when I was thirteen or fourteen years of age. While the bowl was going round they took hold of one anothers hands, and whirling round as in a dance, they sang the ditty, "*Open your mouths and gallop it in, gallop it in*". Though young, I thought how much it is like a wild African dance, for they sent up their legs in the most ridiculous manner. Sometimes men and boys accompanied the hounds to the other side of the Moor Cock Inn, where the huntsman threw off the dogs for a farewell hunt. A hare was quickly started in one of the rough pastures, and after a short but smart chase was killed. That was the signal for a friendly parting until they would meet again.

On our way home the whole company called at the Moor Cock for something to drink. The landlady that morning had baked a batch of riddle bread which had been hung upon the bread fleak to harden. While she was in another part of the house, some young men who were pressed with hunger began to pull the cakes off the fleak, and in a very short time the whole batch disappeared. The landlady, who was a kindly body, took it all in good part. When I was a mere lad I was the most ardent follower of the hounds in the village, and thought that being a huntsman was before all other pursuits in life. In my early boyhood, when the late John King of Clapham and others kept hounds, I would run away to follow them. To hear the chorus of the hounds when in full pursuit, I thought the finest music that could charm my ears.

A change came over me in my young manhood, when I felt the force and beauty of that divine saying, "*Blessed are the merciful, for they shall obtain mercy*". After this change of thought and feeling I could no more join in hunting a hare than in hunting a man. I may mention a singular occurrence at one of the Catherine hunts when I was a lad just in my teens.

On the east side of Lowther Hill farm the hounds lost the hare, and in trying to recover the scent got somewhat scattered. I was alone in an old lane leading from the Clapham road to Wennington Moss, when five or six hounds started the hare, and when it was coming through the hedge one of the dogs caught it as the other dogs came behind. I got down into the ditch, got the head and body of the hare under my left arm and knocked the dogs away with my right hand. Getting the hare free I carried it to where there were some men, when a big mechanic over from Leeds to do repairs at the Mill, seized it by its hind legs, wrenched it from my arms, and killed it. No doubt the hare was exhausted, or it would not have been so easy for a lad to rescue it; but it was very remarkable that the dogs did not attempt to get it from me.

The Coronation of George the Fourth

The coronation, which took place on July 19th, 1821, did not cause much excitement at Bentham more than keeping it a partial holiday. The Bentham Band played at Mr. Overend's, Mr. Roughsedge's, &c., and then went to the festival at Halsteads, near Ingleton. There was a very large gathering, and the festivities were on a large scale. The Rev. T. H. Foxcroft was so excited, shouting and running from one group of people to another, that to me he looked like a man out of his mind. His demonstrative loyalty was of such an uproarious character that many people said he would do himself bodily harm. Though I knew nothing of the disagreement between the King and Queen Caroline, I heard bystanders say that Mr. Foxcroft was very much against her. I have heard the loyal shouts of the Londoners when the Queen was in procession to the House of Commons, and of the French when in the presence of their King, but I never saw a man so full of enthusiasm as the late Mr. Foxcroft. It was beginning to be dusk before the festivities closed by the band playing "*God save the King*". I, a lad of eight years of age, knowing nothing of ceremonial loyalty, unwittingly kept my head covered, when Mr. Foxcroft came running to me and violently knocked my hat off. Mr. Foxcroft died a few months after his great loyal demonstration, when it was said that his death was hastened by his coronation excitement. Mr. Foxcroft was a highly respected and benevolent clergyman, but his loyalty on that day was uncontrollable. An extract from the "*Lonsdale Magazine*" may be added: "*The Rev. Thomas Hammond Foxcroft, of Halsteads, near Kirkby Lonsdale, died on the 8th of October, 1821, in the 57th year of his age. Mr. Foxcroft was a man of irreproachable character, whose conduct as a man threw a lustre round his functions as a minister of the gospel. He was a man of extensive learning, an orthodox preacher, and was himself a living example of the doctrines he taught. Of him it might be said, in the words of Chaucer, Christ's love and His apostles twelve he taught; but first he followed it himself*".

Barring Out at the Grammar School at Christmas

Barring out at the Grammar School was to the boys the most stirring event of the year. There was a good deal of noise and running up and down in the school, but the masters generally let the lads have much of their own way. At one time they supplied a little ale to make it look like Christmas, but never to excess. The illumination of the high school was a very exciting affair. All the scholars were expected to take one pound of candles each. As there was a chandler's shop at Low Bentham, some of the boys of the village took a pride in getting very thick candles for the occasion. Some of them were two in a pound. For candlesticks the boys provided themselves with potatoes and clay. It took a considerable time to make these materials into candlesticks, and to fill them with candles, and place them in rows in front of the school windows. The illumination took place very early in the morning, sometimes before the people were going to their work at the mill. It was a busy time to light so many candles so as to have them all lighted at once. There was hurrahing when the illumination was at its best, and when it was seen from the street it was a grand display, and the lads were excited above measure. It may be readily believed that such a large number of candles burning at once would soon make the school uncomfortably warm. It was a rule to put the candles out when they began to fall through extreme heat. The masters claimed the remains of unburnt candles.

Shrove Tuesday at the School

At one time cocks were fought on Shrove Tuesday, but in lieu of this the scholars were required to bring a cock-penny. The masters expected at the least that each scholar should take a shilling. Some of the boys, whose parents were in better circumstances, would take 2s. 6d., or 5s. The master in return used to give two prizes in books, which were won by throwing dice, but they were never of much value. I was lucky as it was called in winning first prizes twice, one of which was *"The new pleasing instructor"*, and a small Church Prayer Book. The Prayer Book was the second prize, but I had to take it, as the first prize was considered too hard for me to read. There are a few more old customs which are amongst the things of the past, but these reminiscences have so far extended beyond my expectations that I must now say, *"A Happy New Year to those who have read them"*. If they have been of interest to my Bentham friends and others they have also afforded me a pleasant task in living my task over again.

BENTHAM.

Henry Slinger,

SLATER AND PLASTERER,

Wholesale and Retail Dealer in Slates, Ridges, Chimney Tops, Plaster Laths, Nails, Hair, Cement, Plaster of Paris, Sanitary Ware, &c.

H. S. has also taken the Agency for this District of BLACKMORE & CO, Stodehouse Marble Works, Dent, for all kinds of Marble Headstones and Fireplaces. &c. Designs, samples of Stone, and Prices on application. (170

Half-year ending Sept. 31 1872

Mr. Knowles

To the HIGH BENTHAM GAS CO., LIMITED, Dr.

This Account is due on delivery, and must be paid before the end of the present month to

OLIVER BOWKER, Secretary, High Bentham.

To 2,117 Cubic feet of Gas consumed by Meter, at 6/8 per 1000 Cubic Feet	14	
To Meter Rent, &c.	1	
To Arrears		

Settled Jany 15th 1872 £ 15 0

This invoice of 1872 was presented very early in the life of the High Bentham Gas Company. Today's price for Mr. Knowles' consumption of gas would have shown an increase from 14/- (70p) to over £31.

PERSONAL RECOLLECTIONS OF LOWER BENTHAM FROM 1822

No.1 (6th March, 1897)

Early 19th Century New Buildings

It may not be without interest to the present inhabitants to learn something of their predecessors of over seventy years ago. Since that day many changes have taken place by deaths, and the removal of families to Lancaster and other towns. The village, as to its buildings, like Higher Bentham and other small neighbouring towns, until recent date was of very small growth. Until 1820 there did not appear a single house that might have been called a new one, until John Davidson built two neat cottages coming out of Lower Bentham eastward. No houses in that direction have been built since, with the exception of one made out of some outbuildings at the road side leading to Higher Bentham, and at the distance of a hundred yards from Davidson's Cottages, consequently the two Benthams are little nearer to each other than what they were in the last century.

The late Richard Marshall built a good house between the two Benthams and added to it a large market garden. The field was sold to him by Parson Butler on easy terms, so that he might make a more comfortable livelihood, and under more favourable circumstances than working at the High Mill Bleach Works. Marshall's grounds are a little over midway between the two villages. Seventy years ago, or more, John Titterington, master maltster, Lower Bentham, bought Moon's Acre, which is much nearer Higher Bentham than Marshall's gardens, on which he built a good house, with other substantial outbuildings, for carrying on malt-making, &c. This trade, with that of spirit making, collapsed many years ago, and the grounds &c. have been formed into the Bentham Grammar School, and the headmaster's house. After the new malt kiln and the other premises were completed, the old malt kiln and outbuildings at Lower Bentham were made into neat cottages.

The other new buildings to bring the two Benthams to a nearer junction, are a house, market garden &c., opposite the Grammar School, and a cottage made out of a Primitive Methodist Chapel, and a Roman Catholic Day-school, nearer Higher Bentham. The inhabitants of the Lower village show no inclination to extend their borders on the east side and their neighbours in the Upper village are the same as to extending theirs on the west, so that there is little probability of a junction of the two villages ever taking place.

Some Leading Inhabitants

Amongst the leading inhabitants of Lower Bentham there were the Rev. Archdeacon Butler, Rector of Bentham, the Rev. Richard Skirrow (curate), Mr.

Bateson, Ellergill Lodge, Mr. Ellershaw, Stone-gate, Mr. Wm. Green, Mr. James Wallace, Mr. John Altham (surgeon), Mr. C. Thornborrow and Mr. J. Kendal. Over seventy years ago, the inhabitants of the two Benthams who were in more favourable circumstances than tradespeople and the working classes, were generally spoken of as *"The quality"*. At that time Parson Butler was a very old man, and past ministerial and pastoral labour. He was a kind-hearted Rector, and lenient of the poorer classes of farmers as to their tithes. In his old age, when infirmities pressed heavily upon him, his nephew, the Rev. Thomas Butler, who resided at Ridding, did occasional duty for him.

Mr. Thomas Butler, Junior

Mr. Thomas Butler, junior, is not mentioned with any intention to reflect on the National Church, though he was a grief to his venerable and kind-hearted uncle, and little credit to his clerical profession. Drink, which has been a disgrace to Nonconformist ministers as well as clergymen, was his besetting sin, and when under its potent influence his pugilistic propensities were often aroused. The reason for giving this Rev. gentleman a place in these recollections, is that he was a clergyman of rare oratorical powers. Though his face at times showed traces of his bacchanalian follies, still his language, manner and earnestness were so commanding, forcible and pathetic that the attention of the people was absorbed in his discourse and falling tears showed what a mighty spell he had over his congregation. When most eloquent his arms moved with great rapidity, and when he was under great excitement, in a stentorian voice he would exclaim, *"You must do as I say, and not as I do"*.

After his uncle's death he removed to another county, where a change for the better took place. Seventy years ago it was a common thing to hear the father tell to a younger generation the magic influence he had over his congregation. It was a common saying at the time that there was not a preacher, even in London, who could surpass him in pulpit oratory.

Other Rectors of Bentham

The Rev. Archdeacon Butler, rector of Bentham and Whittington, died April 26th, 1825. He was succeeded in the Rectorship by the Rev. Mr. Parker, who was a non-resident, and if ever he did visit his parishioners for their spiritual benefit, his visits were like the angel's visits, few and far between. The Rev. R. Skirrow for many years acted as curate for Mr. Parker. He was a close reader of his sermons and invariably kept his eyes on his manuscript. He had none of the fire of Mr. Thomas Butler, but still his sermons were much appreciated by many of his congregation. He was a kind-hearted gentleman, and gave much away to the poor. If report was correct, he did not look well after his paltry salary, but indeed, whether he was paid or not, it made no difference with his ministry and pastoral duties. His chief concern was for the spiritual welfare of his flock. When he ceased to be curate he retired to his patrimonial estate at Wray.

The Village Doctor

One of the most active and useful men in the village was Doctor Altham, who lived in the house occupied as the Sun-dial Inn. The name is derived from an old sundial fixed above the front door. The Doctor had a very wide practice, including the two Benthams, and during the day he was generally *"on the trot"* on his little cob. He was the only doctor in the neighbourhood until about 1821, when a young doctor of the name of Burrow, who had served his time with Dr. Sellars of Ingleton, opened a practice in Upper Bentham. When he considered himself properly established in his new practice, he married Miss Holmes, the elder daughter of Mr. Thomas Holmes, who was formerly Master of the Grammar School at Wray. The event is more easily remembered because Mr. Morphet, the head master of Collingwood's Grammar School, Upper Bentham, gave us (that is his Upper and Lower Bentham scholars) a holiday, as he was one of the invited guests to the wedding.

Mr. Burrow's stay at Bentham was only of a short duration and his next removal was to Settle, where there was a more favourable opening. This left the two villages to Dr. Altham and his sons for a considerable number of years, before any other doctor opened a practice at either of the Benthams. Mr. James Farrer, the village schoolmaster, had only the smaller boys of the village under his tuition, as the bigger lads generally attended the Upper Bentham Grammar School. Christopher Thornborrow may be mentioned as one of the gentry, who, as a retired tradesman, lived on his means. He, like many more of the villagers, was ardently fond of John Barleycorn; spirits were not so much in use at that day as they are now. He frequently preferred a walk to Upper Bentham for his refreshments to his own village inn, the Punch Bowl. He was one of the best tempered men, whether drunk or sober. It was amusing to see him on such occasions, walk down the street on his way home. Though he was sure to be talking to passers by, or to himself, he always maintained the best of tempers. The way in which he walked was as good as a show. He reeled first from one side of the street to the other, so that he measured the distance many times over before he reached his home. His eyes were incessantly opening and shutting, his arms and fingers were kept moving in all manners of directions, as if he was engaged in some pantomimic performance.

The Village Tradesmen

From 1824, and for many years subsequently, the tradesmen were not numerous. Robert Foster and Benjamin Cocking were blacksmiths; Robert Ward, draper; Christopher Johnson, tallow chandler; Jonathan Redmayne, mason; John Titterington, maltsman; John Tatham, butcher; John Townson, hatter; James Wilcock, cabinet-maker and licensed victualler, Punch Bowl Inn; Peter Blezard, James Clapham, John Cumberland, Thomas Dowbiggin and Thomas Wrathall, carpenters; Hornby & Co., flax and tow spinners; John Kendal, flax-dresser; and James Gibson Carter, James Bateson and William Smith, drapers and grocers. There were a few shoemakers of the name of Thornton, and some tailors who worked in their own houses. The tailors did a deal of work at the houses of their customers, at one shilling and one and sixpence a day, and their meat. In the course of time, other tradesmen came and opened shops. Ted (Edward) Foster, in addition to keeping a shop for general goods, took in weaving for Messrs. Waithman, and put it out to weavers in the village and neighbourhood. The High Mill Company also put out a little linen weaving in the village, but the weaving business collapsed before most of the present inhabitants were born.

A few notices of some of the old tradesmen of the village may not be out of place. About 1822, Robert Ward was a rising and plodding tradesman in the drapery business. At this date it was usual for most of the country drapers to go certain rounds in the district with a pack well stored with goods, so that in time they became well known and respected as itinerant tradesmen. Eventually he bought the old smithy in Upper Bentham, opposite the workhouse, and the adjoining cottages. The premises, which were fitted up for carrying on an extensive village and country drapery business, &c., soon became, by tact and fair dealing, the principal shopping mart in the district. The business a few years ago passed into the possession of Mr. Thomas Procter.

I have a vivid recollection of a sad event taking place when I was a boy, which was that of one of the tradesmen taking away his own life. He was a remarkably quiet and good-natured man, and in good circumstances, but drink was his besetting sin, and it was the chief cause of his tragical end. This case is mentioned more than anything else to show what a strange superstition still lingered in the district as to a cure for cancer. A poor woman at Ingleton, who had been persuaded to believe that if a cancer was touched with the hand of a suicide it would heal it, went all the way to Lower Bentham for this purpose. When she had told her errand, the relatives said that though they did not think such a thing would do her any good, still she was quite welcome to try it. Though the poor woman was pleased with her friendly reception, and returned home with cheerful hopes for the better, still her cancer proved fatal.

John Cumberland and Spirits

John Cumberland was one of the notorieties of the village. He could see visions, foretell deaths, and other remarkable things, or at the least, he had acquired a name for the discerning of spirits. He was a man of gentle and mild temper, and far from being quarrelsome even when under the influence of drink. He, like many of his neighbours, frequently came to Upper Bentham for refreshments. It used to be reported that one dark night, when returning home, and had reached Kill Dub, some evil sprite dragged him through a high quick-thorn hedge on the east side of Moon's Acre, and then over hedge and dyke, and left him bewildered, with his clothes nearly torn off his back, to find his way home. This may appear to many persons incredible but still it would arise from something that had taken place. The following is likely to be the origin of it. The man had taken too much drink and as the night was very dark, he reeled into the torn hedge, and, as he could not regain his feet, he struggled through to the other side, when he found himself in a worse plight than when in the road. One may well imagine how, in this condition, he would walk round a field until he could find his way through another hedge or hedges, until the dawn of day, so that when he arrived at home his clothes would be tattered and torn. I believe this was the case, and it was an easy matter, at that day, to attribute such things to the evil one, or some of his race. It was said that he used to sit in the Parish Church all night on All Hallowe'en, when he saw the spirits of all the parishioners that would die during the year. He was very nimble in climbing, so that he could, when he pleased, reach the bell ropes through the sounding holes. On such occasions he used to ring the bells at night, to the astonishment of the people in the village. Though such things were said of Cumberland, he was a good neighbour, and was much respected, and his friends were more pleased than vexed with his harmless frolics.

In my youth, many persons believed in the spirits of people being seen who were shortly to die. There was an old woman, nearly eighty years of age, of the name of Thompson, who lived in an old thatched house in Upper Bentham, on the site of which there is now a draper's shop, and opposite to the post office, who was credited with seeing people before they died.

BENTHAM.

THOMAS **P**ROCTER,
DRAPER, &c., THE BEEHIVE,

IS now showing a large Assortment of, ladies and Children's JACKETS, DOLMANS, ULSTERS, &c., in the Newest Designs for SPRING and SUMMER WEAR. A call respectfully solicited.
Agent for John B·rii, Dyer, &c. [737

No.2 (13th March, 1897)

The Parish Clerks

Amongst the noticeable men of Lower Bentham were the parish clerks, who considered themselves next in order to the parson. In reading the psalms in public worship it was the invariable custom for the parson and the clerk to read alternately verse for verse, and for the clerk in all the prayers to give all the responses. The congregation took no other part than that of silently following by looking at their prayer books, and the same order was followed when the choir sang the Psalms by Sternhold and Hopkins. It was seldom that hymns were sung at that day with the exception of two by Bishop Ken, "*Awake my soul*", in the morning service, and "*Glory to Thee my God*", at the afternoon service. Evening services in country churches and hymn singing are of a modern date.

The oldest parish clerk that I can remember was an old man of the name of Thornton, who lived in a small cottage in Higher Bentham, which stood on the site of the Friends' Meeting House. It is nearly eighty years since he died, when his son Thomas removed to Kirkby Lonsdale, where he established a good shoe-making business, which was carried on with success to the close of his life and that of his son Thomas. The Thorntons were leading singers at Beck Lane Chapel, and young Thomas, as he was called, was a noted musician and one of the leaders in Kirkby Lonsdale band in 1843. He was also one of the leading dahlia growers in the district, and with the late Mr. Isaac Hindson and Mr. Hutchinson and Mr. James (who still lives hale and hearty, and as busy as in his younger days in all matters concerning the Parish Church and churchyard improvement) were amongst the promoters in getting up the first Kirkby Lonsdale flower show. The only members of the old parish clerk's family still living in Upper Bentham are three granddaughters, Miss Wilson and her sisters.

The succeeding parish clerk at Lower Bentham was William Bond, who retained the office as long as he was able to discharge his duties. One cannot well forget the parish clerk of that day, with his sober look, his hair combed straight down over his forehead, and the way he left his desk for the singing loft, and as he walked down the aisle in a fine musical voice intoned the words, *"Let us sing to the praise and glory of God the 103rd Psalm"*. There are few parsons still living who can remember how common it was for the clerk at the end of the morning service to hasten out of the church and mount a tombstone at the south entrance of the church when the people gathered around him to hear what sales or notices he had to *"call"*. Public sales, nut or hazel woods when nuts were becoming ripe, and anything of public interest was advertised in this vocal manner by the parish clerk. It was usual for farmers and others who had not attended morning service to enquire of those who had, *"Did t'clerk coo ought today?"* Without justifying this method of advertising sales, &c., one may say that country or village printing had not come into use, and as to newspapers, very few were circulated on account of their high price. If one or two came into a village, perhaps half-a-dozen readers would join at a single one. The public inns would take one each for the benefit of their customers. It is stated that at the beginning of the present century there was only one newspaper published in Lancashire, and that was a Liverpool paper. Another was printed at Whitehaven in Cumberland, and one at Leeds, consequently advertising in the way mentioned was adopted.

Funeral Arrangements

It will be of some interest to younger generations to know how the parish clerk conducted funerals. As a rule in both villages all the funerals were carried out with much piousness and with becoming economy. With very few exceptions there were no hearses. The only funeral I remember up to 1835 when there was an unusual train of carriages and less showy vehicles, was the funeral of Mr. Johnson, of Grove Hill, Upper Bentham. The general custom was to carry the dead on a bier shoulder high, which was followed by the parish clerk, the relatives of the dead and their friends. The clerk attended every funeral, and when the friends were ready for starting he gave out Dr. Watts' doleful hymn, *"Thee we adore eternal name"*, when he took the lead in singing. He had a very solemn way of intoning the two lines, which he gave out at once, so that those who wished to join in the solemn dirge might not have too great a strain on their memories.

The Square, Low Bentham, with the Co-operative Society store on the left and the Victoria Institute which was opened in 1905 as a Public Hall and an Institute. Since 1871 the village had enjoyed a News Room, complete with rooms for reading, smoking and bagatelle.

It was very impressive even to a youngster like myself when he slowly intoned, in his sonorous musical voice, "*Our wasting lives grow shorter still as days and months increase*". When the funerals were from Upper Bentham, the singing was continued to the end of the village, and the same custom was followed at Lower Bentham. On many occasions the singing was left to the clerk, so that in course of time the old custom passed away.

One reason why nut woods were called in the Churchyard on a Sunday morning after Church service with threatenings of law to trespassers was that lads and young men were very troublesome to farmers who intended to gather their nuts for their own use or for sale. An instance will show how many of the farmers were treated in protecting their crop of nuts. There was a family of the name of Whitehead who lived at Escewbeck farm, which was not far from Wilcock's Punch Bowl Inn, and on the road leading to Tatham Moor, where they had some nut woods. They had much trouble in protecting them when the nuts were becoming ripe, especially on Sunday afternoons. Many of the young men gathered in the lane between two woods, some of them for a frolic as much as to gather nuts. Hearing of these Sunday afternoon gatherings, I, with some other Upper Bentham lads, went on one occasion to see the rows. It was surprising to see the large number of lads and young men who had come together either to get nuts or to make game out of the Whitehead family. The same still lingers vividly in my memory just as it took place. There were old Tommy and his wife, and young Tommy and his two sisters standing on a brow outside of a wood on the left side of the road leading into Tatham. From this eminence they had a good view over the wood, so that no one could pass in or out without being seen. Then young men over and again shouted, "*See, Tommy, they've gitten into t'wood, and they're pulling t'nuts off as fast as they can*", and other words of a similar character. This kind of teasing went on for some time, to the evident annoyance of the Whiteheads. To me it is a pleasing reflection that I took no part in teasing the members of one of the quietest families in the neighbourhood. Certainly according to English law I was culpable for being in the crowd.

When I used to sit in the Parish Church as a Sunday scholar the Misses Whitehead often passed me. They were tall, and of a slim figure, and as straight as an arrow. Their garments were plain, and much behind what was called "*the fashion*". Evidently they did not care for ever-changing modes of dress, for they showed more regard for plainness in their attire than a wasteful and vain show. What used to puzzle my boyish mind was that always before they entered their pew in the Parish Church each of them stood and made a courtesy. This was no more puzzling than to see men as soon as they entered their pews turn their heads to the pulpit and look into their hats before they sat down. No doubt it was rather simple of me, when I was first taken to the Church as a small Sunday scholar, to ask my father why men put their faces into their hats.

General Election

There was a shoemaker of the name of Thornton who once did a plucky thing at a general election, which at the time brought him favourably into public notice. He was pretty well known previously in the two villages and the surrounding neighbourhood. He was much given to cultivating flowers and various sorts of shrubs, and when he heard of anyone getting a new plant of any sort which he had not in his garden he was sure to visit the owner that he might have the pleasure of examining it. On account of this fondness of flowers and other plants, he was generally spoken of as Myrtle Bobby. It was an inoffensive name, and was not used with any disrespect. Plants and flowers were his hobby, and the myrtle, from ancient times, had always been a fancy plant. He married rather late in life, after which he came into possession of an annual £2 property franchise. At this time there were few farmers and workingmen, or even tradesmen, who had county votes and those who had were chiefly Tories. The Whigs were a very small minority, and as for such terms as Liberal and Conservative, they had not come into use. The Tories, who were a large majority, professed to be zealous supporters of Church and State, and consequently they looked upon the Whigs as semi-traitors to the Throne.

At a general election, when the poll took place at Settle, Myrtle Bobby decided to maintain his colour, and march boldly to the poll. He was determined that he would not be deterred by the overwhelming number of political opponents. There was no ballot box to shield timid voters at that day, and Robert had no connection with such a class. Carriages were not much in vogue at that date, especially for Whigs. He had a tidy and light cart, to which he attached his two donkeys, gay with yellow favours. Whip and rein in hand, amid many lookers-on, he mounted his carriage and started off with the crack of his whip to the delight of his friends. There were shouts of *"Well done, Robert, you're not afraid of showing your colour"*. He had over 12 miles to go, and he was never so popular as he was that day. As he passed through the two villages there were roars of merriment and laughter. Many encouraging words he received on his journey, and hearty were his greetings. Though hundreds of people came to use the donkey tandem, they were on the side of the Whigs. When the donkeys entered Settle with their flying colours there was excited interest and wonderment. Though there were some persons who could not but frown and say *"What has that chap come to do?"*, there were others who shouted *"Well done, Bobby, we honour you for your pluck"*. Robert was proud of his independence that day, and felt glad that he had the opportunity of openly recording his vote in favour of political freedom.

An Old Soldier

There was an old Waterloo trooper in the village, called Neddy (Edward) Camm, who came in for a little more than usual respect on account of his having been in that famous battle, which was the fatal step in the downfall of Napoleon I. He was like most pensioners of that date, too fond of drink, and when under the influence he was often teased, even to excitement. In the battle his horse was killed under him, and he was shot by a musket ball in the chin, the mark of which was very visible under the lower lip. His voice was also effected from the effect the bullet had had on the lower gum. When he was fresh, young men and boys used to say, *"Neddy, when thee was shot thee was liggin' behind thy horse, when tha' popped thy head up , and t' bullet catched thy chin*". Neddy must have been a fine looking soldier when he was in full uniform because he was tall and of an excellent figure. I only remember two old soldier pensioners - Neddy and Tom Heaton of Upper Bentham who had been wounded in battle. His speech was affected similarly to Neddy's, which was most likely from similar circumstances, by the appearance of his chin.

Hat Makers

One of the old trades of Lower Bentham, hat making, was carried on by a family of the name of Townson. This, like the same business which was carried on by the Tennants and Skirrows, of Upper Bentham, is a thing of the past. It may be remarked that one William Thornton, a member of an old Lower Bentham family, carried his hat making to Kirkby Lonsdale. He was living in the main street in 1843, but at that date the business was a thing of the past. Mrs. Metcalfe (generally called *"Jinny"*) a native of Lower Bentham, and sister of William, was a well known woman, plain of speech, and one who had a mind of her own. John Metcalfe, her son, a highly respected man, was up to his death the actuary of Kirkby Lonsdale Savings Bank.

SANDERSON'S,
DRAPERS, HOSIERS, &c.

FASHIONABLE MILLINERY
AND
DRESSMAKING ESTABLISHMENT,
MARKET PLACE, BENTHAM.

NOTE.— Opposite the Town Hall. A call will oblige.

No.3 (20th March, 1897)

Short Biographical Notices of Boys who Attended Collingwood Grammar School: The Altham Family

It is somewhat difficult to make out the subsequent career of many of the scholars who went to the Higher Bentham Grammar School, as they in early life removed with their families to other towns. Amongst the earliest boys I recollect were Dr. Altham's boys, who were named Robert, John, William, James, and Thomas. John and Robert, who I believe were twins, were remarkably fine looking men when they reached their full manhood. After leaving their father they opened a medical practice at Hornby. Eventually John, who married the only daughter of Lawrence Thornton of Burton-in-Lonsdale (and the niece of Richard Thornton, the London millionaire who at considerable expense founded the Burton-in-Lonsdale schools), took up his residence in that village, where he lived during his life. As is usual with doctors, he was frequently out late at night when attending to his outside patients, and as a matter of course when boggarts and spirits were more commonly seen than they are in this enlightened age, he had some strange experiences.

I remember one instance which was very much discussed by the villagers, that took place about 1840. Such a case was well calculated to frighten naughty boys who stay out of doors to a late hour in the streets. The night was very dark on one occasion, but very suitable for the pranks of a village dobby when the doctor was returning from seeing his outside patients. Somewhere about Jogging Bridge, near Ireby, the dobby appeared all of a sudden, which frightened the doctor's horse into a gallop, and nearly unseated its rider. The faster the horse sped its way homewards, the more furiously the dobby rattled his chains and pursued its victims. The descent of the very steep brow near Thwaitber, was accomplished in a trice, and the wonder was how the horse kept its feet and the rider his seat. Happily both man and beast entered the village just in the nick of time, because dobbies always shrink when there is either daylight or candlelight. According to report the horse was lathered with sweat, but it was well that nothing more harmful took place to it or its rider than a good fright. Some persons may laugh at the folly of believing in dobbies or boggarts, but when I was a lad it was a common thing to believe in them.

There was one at Gooda, between Burton-in-Lonsdale and Ingleton. One night, in my time, an Ingletonian, well primed with drink, encountered this flaying, as it was called, and still believed in by some persons who would not dare to pass the place in the dark. The inebriate was so alarmed that he took to his heals and ran until he was quite exhausted, when he stopped and said, "*Good Divil thou mun tak' ma*". Both of the brothers Altham spent their days one at Wray and the other at Burton-in-Lonsdale. They were of genial temperament, unassuming and friendly to their patients and friends. The Altham's, on the mother's side, are of an old Quaker family, and her son John was buried in the Friends' burial ground, Calf-cop, Lower Bentham.

William Altham, sometime after his father's death, removed to Upper Bentham, where he carried on a successful practice for many years. He married for his first wife Miss Taylor, the daughter of a Lancashire gentleman who was manager of the Higher Bentham Flax Mill. Doctor William was nothing near as tall and robust as the two brothers mentioned. He was well liked by the tradesmen and the working class. There was nothing about him proud and haughty, and no doubt it was his uniform geniality which made him a special favourite with the mothers and their children. Eventually he removed to Settle, where he was much respected, and where, I believe, he ended his days. James was a pupil with the late Doctor Wildman of Wray. Early on in life he went to the West Indies, and if he is still living, will be 80 years of age or more. Thomas, the youngest son, went to his uncle at Penrith, where he was brought up to the trade of an ironmonger. After his uncle's death he succeeded to the business in which, the last time I was at Penrith, he was doing a good business, and was highly respected as a tradesman. The family name, once so notable at Lower Bentham, has entirely passed from the neighbourhood.

Christopher Thornborrow and Christmas Candles

The sons of Christopher Thornborrow, tallow chandler, have all departed this life many years ago. William died just when he was rising to young manhood. Giles, the youngest, was an apprentice with Christopher Johnson, tallow chandler, who was successor to his father. The premises were up a yard near the Temperance Hotel and boarding houses kept by Miss Leeming. It was at this shop where the bigger boys with the aid of Giles Thornborrow made unusual sized candles for the Christmas candle illumination in the Upper Grammar School. It was said that some of them were a pound weight each. Every scholar was expected to take one pound of candles or more, and it was fine fun to make clay and potato candlesticks and fix the candles in them for the illumination. The candles were placed on the window sills or on at other place which would add to the brilliancy of the exhibition.

The boys from Lower Bentham, as well as those of Higher Bentham, had to be at the school by 6 a.m., soon after which a brilliant glare was shed on the school hill, the street, and on the front of the Royal Oak Inn. One may be sure that on account of the heat radiating from such a great number the room would be almost unbearable. As soon as the candles began to bow their heads that was the notice to put them out. During the illumination the boys shouted and hurrahed as if they were beside themselves. This was to show that they were overjoyed because the illumination was the forerunner of a month's holiday.

Giles Thornborrow, long before serving his time out to the drudgery of tallow chandler, came to the possession of his deceased uncle's property in the Fylde, sometime after which he married Miss Toulman of Grove Hill, Upper Bentham. The eldest son of Mr. C. Thornborrow was brought up to the law, and eventually for his second wife he married Mrs. Altham of Burton-in-Lonsdale, where he spent his days. There were other boys named Whitehead, Townson, Lord, Bateson, and a William Cumberland, who died when he was rising to young manhood.

Christoper Thompson

One of the more notable lads amongst the Lower Bentham scholars for his diligent application to his school work was Christopher Thompson. His father lived on a farm at the north end of the village where a footway leads to the Lancaster road near the Parish Church. I believe his father lived on his own land, and was one of the few yeomen who at that date held such a position at Lower Bentham. Christopher Thompson and I were born in the month of December, I on the 3rd, and he on the 5th, 1813. He was the second elder son of a family of thirteen members. He was very successful in his studies, and in due time he was sent to Giggleswick Grammar School, at which time his father intended to make him a lawyer. From Giggleswick he was sent to St. Bees, with the object of becoming a clergyman of the Church of England. On leaving St. Bees he was ordained deacon to Giggleswick Parish.

After being ordained priest he removed to Tynemouth Priory, and from thence to Walker-on-the-Tyne, Northumberland, where he laboured usefully and peaceably to the end of his days. Mr. Thompson, in 1850, married the widow of the late William Mountain of Benton Hall, by whom he had two children, a son and a daughter. Mr. Thompson, when he was at school, was of a quiet and peaceable temper, and he was more devoted to his studies than many of the other boys, who were too fond of quarrelling and provoking battles, which was generally egged on by lads who preferred seeing a fight to being engaged in one. It appears that as he grew in years the mild temperament of his youth served him well, and also his parishioners in his riper years. It was said that he was greatly loved by the various religious bodies in his parish whether they were Catholic or Protestant. He had the good word of all his neighbours and friends, and a localism of frequent use in his declining years was, "*He is a canny old man*". This localism would carry more weight in Northumberland than in his native village. Mr. Thompson died in August, 1881, and was buried in Walker Churchyard, where he reposes in peace amongst many of his parishioners. In the following year a beautiful memorial window was erected at the east end of the Church, the title of which was, "*The good Samaritan*". Such a testimony of clerical worth must be very pleasing to any branches of the Thompson family still remaining in Lower Bentham, and to any of the old people who remember the lad when he daily walked between two and three miles to Collingwood Grammar School.

As to Mr. Thompson's children, his son died at Madiera, and the daughter still lives in the house in which she was born, and is now a mother. This very singular business is now accounted for, the Rev. A. S. Wardroper (who succeeded Mr. Thompson) having married Miss Thompson. It is not a bad wish to say, may he, after a long and useful ministry, acquire the public testimony of his father-in-law, "*He is a canny old man*".

Doctor Jackson

Doctor Jackson may appropriately follow the Rev. C. Thompson, as they were cousins. As a lad he was brought up with his uncle, James Gibson Carter, who kept a grocer and draper's shop a little out of the village on the north side. The uncle was an active business man and was for a long course of years the overseer of the poor. Thomas Jackson after passing through various courses of study, was admitted into one of the London colleges. I remember speaking at a temperance meeting at Slaidburn, some years before he died, when he was present. He invited me to spend an hour with him at his lodgings. He was not married and he died a bachelor. In my remarks I mentioned that the continued use of beer had such an injurious effect upon draymen that the scratch of a nail or a slight abrasion of the skin was often fatal. The doctor referred to this remark and said that he had many proofs of its truth when he walked the hospitals. He was a kindly and jolly conversationalist, and an inveterate smoker of tobacco. He was a big man and of shapely mould, and he presented a good appearance either as a rider or pedestrian. His useful medical career ended somewhat suddenly. He had a presentiment that he would not live to a long age, and only a few weeks before the end came he said to Mr. G. Parker (Colleyholme), one of his patients, "George I shall die before thee." His friend is still living hale and active, advancing towards the 80th year of his age.

The doctor died July 25th, 1872, in the 62nd year of his age, and was buried at the Parish Church, Lower Bentham, July 30th. He was very much respected in the district where he had practised, as was proved by the attendance and feeling of those who witnessed the funeral cortege as it left his residence for Lower Bentham Church. For some unaccountable reason the corpse only received scant courtesy on its arrival at the Churchyard. The late Dr. Elletson, who married for his second wife one of Dr. Jackson's cousins, was the first to greet the funeral cortege. The doctor's patients were forbidden admission into the church and they had to remain in the churchyard during the first part of the burial service. The reason for the scant attendance of friends might be because there were few who remembered Tommy Jackson in his schoolboy days. As a doctor he was universally liked in his district, and many of the old people often say, *"We wish the old doctor was back again"*.

Successful medical men in a wide and sparse district have usually not much time on their hands, but when such occasions occurred the doctor devoted them to angling, for as a fisher with a rod he was very successful in the neighbouring rivers. He excelled in botany, and took much pleasure in the study of birds, their habits, nests and their eggs. He was an excellent pedestrian, and when the weather was favourable, he would in one direction walk seven miles to Whitewell, and in the other direction five miles to Tosside Chapel to see his patients, whilst his horse was resting in the stable. When leisure allowed he indulged in reading old literature, Latin mottoes and inscriptions over the doors of old houses, in fact nothing came wrong if it was worth attending to. His successor, Dr. Sinclair, who was his pupil in 1865, is still following up some of Dr. Jackson's old practice.

Bought of THOMAS MARSHALL,
Complete House Furnisher.

BRASS AND IRON BEDSTEADS, SPRING, HAIR, AND STRAW MATTRASSES, FEATHER AND FLOCK BEDS.

CARPETS, LINOLEUMS, AND FLOOR OIL CLOTHS.

AGENT FOR THE END OVER END, BARREL AND OTHER CHURNS.

WASHING AND WRINGING MACHINES, SEWING MACHINES, ETC.

FUNERALS FURNISHED.

This billhead shows that the outward appearance of Hash Browns on Main Street has changed little over the last 100 years. Straw mattresses and sewing machines were available - as well as the furnishing of funerals.

No.4 (27th March, 1897)

Fire at the Holmes

As in the following narrative the old mill fire-engine will become a noticeable object it may not be out of place to mention how I identify it with my early boy-hood. It may be seventy-five years ago since a fire broke out in a barn at *"The Holmes"* on the west of the Lower Bentham toll-bar, when the High Mill engine was used to put it out. When it passed through Upper Bentham on its way to the fire, as a matter of course, it caused considerable excitement amongst the boys as well as the adult inhabitants. With other small boys I followed it to the fire. The engine for some reason failed to be of much use as it had done on many subsequent occasions. The fire, after many hours contention with it, was put out, but it was when there was little to burn except the blackened walls. On the return journey John Tempest, the man who was driving the engine, seeing two or three boys on their way to Upper Bentham so tired that he asked them to get on the front of the engine, which was a seat comfortable enough for boys though somewhat dangerous on account of its small wooden wheels, which left but a narrow space between the bottom of the engine and the road. I thoughtlessly allowed my feet to touch the ground, when they caught and as I was being drawn under the engine I called out, when the driver stopped his horse and I escaped being crushed to death. This was the first of my marvellous escapes in a prolonged life.

The Disastrous Fire at Lower Bentham Mill

It must now be somewhere about forty-four years since it took place. On a stone in the restored mill there are the following dates, 1785 - 1852, the first number referring to the date when the mill was first built, and the second when it was rebuilt. On the downspouts there is the date 1852. At the time the fire took place I was over from Kirkby Lonsdale at Upper Bentham when there was a cry from the bottom of the village, *"Low Bentham Mill is on fire"*, which was repeated from one person to another to the east end of the village, and to more distant places. Men, women and children were running in every direction to the scene of the fire, some on the road and some by the fields on the banks of the Wenning. The clerks, hecklers, bleachers, and others were running from the high mill either to see the fire or to help putting it out. The news had quickly spread to Ingleton, and Mr. J. T. Coates and others were amongst the crowd. To me the fire and its surroundings are almost as vividly before my eyes now as they were on the day of their occurrence. There was a large crowd of men, women and children on the lofty brow on the west side of the mill where they were out of danger. Most of the male mill hands appeared confused, and appeared as if they had no heart to make themselves useful.

The fire engine was standing as if nobody knew how to use it. I threw off my coat and hat, and along with Mr. Coates and Joshua Alderson, a clerk at the high mill, we took hold of it to drag it nearer the mill. When passing under a burning beam, which went from one building to another, Mrs. Alderson came and dragged her husband away, saying, "*You will be killed*". My wife was in the crowd of lookers on, but she would not hinder me from doing a work of necessity. When the engine had been put in position men gathered round, either as pumpers or fetchers of water. Whether the engine had been used before my arrival or not I am not able to say. At this time the fire had good hold of the upper storey, which was, I believe, the fourth.

A Man Needed to Fly the Hose

It may be asked where were the trained fire brigade and the leader! There appeared to be none, and the engine and the hose were in a most lamentable condition, a disgrace to any mill company. The confused state of affairs may be understood when I, a stranger and inexperienced, had to take the hose and mount the tall mill ladder. To justify my speaking of myself so much is necessary because while I was present I had to run the greatest risk. When I reached the uppermost window I found that the hose was leaking and the water issued from it with comparatively feeble force. At times the fire was raging furiously, and before I had been long in this position the flames burst through the opening into my feet, and knocked me off the ladder. Happily I was not knocked off sideways or I should have been killed, and while I was sliding down the front of the ladder I caught one of its rungs and re-ascended with the hose still in my hand.

Shortly after I had regained my position I felt that there was someone below me on the ladder. I looked round and saw it was my late brother Isaac. He previously had entreated me to come away from the fire as I might be killed if I did not. Being astonished at his exposing himself to danger I said, "*How is it you are here?*" It appeared that seeing me void of fear aroused his courage, and he said, "*I saw you.*" I soon found that with such a leaky hose it was of little use continuing the struggle, as the mill was a wreck and the fire was burning itself out.

The next thing was to try and save the engine house, as the fire had not got right hold of it. This portion of the premises was on the river side, and it was considerably lower in its construction than the mill. At this state of the fire the hose had become so considerably worse that its only use was to keep a slender flow of water to where the two buildings joined and let it run into the building below. After continuing the work far into the afternoon it was considered safe to put the old fire engine on one side. It would not be just to say it did no good, for the engine house was saved, and it was the only portion of the mill that was not insured. The mill was a total wreck, and it was well that none of the mill cottages took any harm. The saddest thing about the fire was that one of the mill hands was burnt to death. Happily I escaped from any harm except the blackening of my face and the burning of my eyelashes and eyebrows.

The Supposed Origin of the Fire

The fire broke out in the carding room early on in the forenoon. The room in some places was covered with fluffy material from the carding of tow, which was of such a character as to readily take fire from a match or a lighted pipe. One of the hands, an elderly Irish woman who attended to the feeding machine, was guilty of smoking at times, for which she had been frequently reproved. As she denied having been smoking at the time the fire broke out it was supposed that a match had been thrown into some tow and thrown into the spreading engine. The late George Phillipson, who was the carding master, told me that the fire broke out with such a startling suddenness that the whole room in the course of a few minutes was in a blaze. His son, William Phillipson, who is still a resident at Upper Bentham, says that it was not more than two minutes in catching the whole of the most inflammable material in the room, so that the workpeople had little time to escape. The excitement and dread of being burnt was indescribable. Some of the hands who were near the door threw a quantity of laps which were on fire into the stone stair passage, which, kindling into a blaze, became a wall of fire and barred the way of escape to those who were flying from the upper rooms. It may be imagined what was the terror of the workpeople when they saw that their way out of the mill was in a blaze.

Happily there was one way left to escape, and that was through the making up room, and as there was no stairway for their descent they were let down to the mill yard by a rope and pulley. A quiet and inoffensive young woman called Dodgson seeing that the people had to wait for their turns, she said, "*I'll go back and put my bobbings on.*" It was evident that she was particular in seeing that her bobbings were put on in their right position, though the mill was on fire. Being too exact was a fatal step, and when she returned the workpeople had escaped and the rope of the hoist, through the great strain that had been put on it, was broken. Either that night or the next morning her remains when found consisted chiefly of a few charred bones. Much sympathy was felt for the poor girl and her parents.

During the time the mill was being rebuilt many of the hands were employed at the Upper Mill, Bentham. Some years after the mill had been built it was purchased by Mr. T .P. Benson Ford, and the premises were turned into a silk mill. After it came into his hands he put in a new engine and boiler, and made other additions needful for the business and the advantage of the workpeople. About 200 workpeople are employed at the Lower Bentham Mill, and 25 at the Greta Bank Mill at Burton-in-Lonsdale. The work carried on is dressing and spinning waste silk, which is used for making dress goods such as plushes, laces, handkerchiefs, and many other things.

Mr. Robert Wildman, Bank Manager

Some time before the old tow mill was burnt down a portion of it was occupied by a Frenchman who manufactured goods of an ornamental character, consisting of borders, check muslin, and calico, done with gold and silver paint. There was for a time a remarkable young man connected with the works of the name of Robert Wildman. He was a member of an old Methodist family at Settle. He for a time attended Giggleswick Grammar School, where he was a pupil under Mr. Howson, father of the late Dr. Howson, Dean of Chester. He was a remarkably fine singer,

98 PERSONAL RECOLLECTIONS OF LOWER BENTHAM FROM 1822

and for some time which he spent in Leeds he was admitted into the choir of the celebrated Dr. Wesley. I remember meeting him at a temperance festival held in the Bentham Workhouse, either in 1843 or 1844. It was at that time I heard that he was employed under the Frenchman, but in what capacity I did not inquire. He did not remain there long, for some time in 1844 he entered the service of the Craven Banking Company. He afterwards removed to Colne, shortly after which he succeeded, as manager, Mr. Earnshaw, who had resigned through ill-health.

To the end of his life, which took place January 4th 1887, Mr. Wildman retained the management of the bank, to the satisfaction of the Company and all persons who had dealings with it. During Mr. Wildman's forty-three years connection with the Craven Bank he did his duty to himself and his employers with perfect uprightness and integrity. He spent much of his leisure as well as his income in promoting Sunday and week-night schools. In 1886 his numerous friends as a mark of respect unveiled his portrait with this inscription under it. *"This portrait is presented by the Colne Gospel Temperance Blue Ribbon Union as a token of esteem for the services rendered by Mr. and Mrs. Wildman in the great reformation worked in connection with the Iron and Railway-street adult schools, July 17th 1886."* At one time there were 600 members connected with the Iron School. Somewhere about 1885 he decided to give an annual old people's tea, which is still continued. At one of my interviews with him at Colne, I mentioned Ingleton old people's tea which was about to take place, with which he was so pleased that he gave me a subscription towards it.

My last interview with him was after he had a paralysis stroke which had rendered him very feeble. He would have me to go with him just outside the town where he had a favourite resort, that he might have a chat with me on old times. He was a good useful man, and at his funeral his remains were followed by the Colne Local Board, office bearers of the Wesleyan Chapel, teachers and officials of the George-street Wesleyan School, by friends from the Albert Wesleyan Chapel, a large number of scholars from the Iron School, and from other congregations besides the Wesleyans. A Lancashire M.P. said, *"I call to mind what Mr. Wildman was when I first knew him, and what earnestness there was in his settled purpose to serve his generation according to the will of God. I shall ever cherish the memory of his noble, unselfish character, and of his unvarying kindness to me."* A County Magistrate said, *"I shall much regret his loss, as he had become one of my oldest remaining friends at Colne, the town of which owes much to his large benevolence."* Many testimonies of a similar character were borne of his public worth and benevolence. Either villages like the two Benthams or larger manufacturing towns may be well proud that such a man as Mr. Robert Wildman for a time sojourned amongst them, and yet it is likely that few inhabitants of the said villages have much recollection of the youth that dwelt amongst them in 1843.

No.5 (3rd April, 1897)

Village Churches

"Think, when the bells do chime
The angels' music; therefore come not late,
God then deals blessings; if a king did so,
Who would not haste, nay give, to see the show." Herbert

Village churches and *"Church Garths"* are generally looked upon by Nonconformists as well as Churchmen with reverence and affection. No doubt this respect is more deeply rooted in the inhabitants of our villages than in those of large towns. The house of prayer where people have been baptised, confirmed, and married, and their kin have been buried for generations, whatever changes may have taken place in their religious creeds, their reverence for the Parish Church and *"God's acre"* will never change. When we walk amongst the mounds of our departed relatives and friends, and look upon their names inscribed on perishable stone, we cannot resist these tender emotions of Christian love which level all creeds and distinctions, and make us feel in the presence of the dead that it is not beliefs and professions but deeds of mercy and kindness which give worth to the departed and insure to them a hope of the resurrection to eternal life. Apart from creeds, intelligent and enlightened Nonconformists love to linger along the aisles of England's ancient churches, and they have a fine appreciation of the symmetry, beauty and massiveness of Saxon, Norman and early English architecture.

Low Bentham Parish Church

My recollections of the Parish Church are as it stood in 1875, when it was in agitation to have it restored. I visited the old fabric that I might see it as it appeared in my boyhood. Whatever changes may take place in a man's religious views, he cannot but feel a lingering respect for the church of his fathers, and the place where he used to sit as a Sunday scholar.

The exact architecture and the date of the first church no doubt will for ever remain a secret. There was a church of a very early date, and the first mention of it, though remarkably brief, is in Domesday Book. This book was begun by the order of William the Conqueror in 1080, and completed in 1086. The record is thus made:- *"Manors. Wennington, Tatham, Farlton, and Tunstal Chetel had four manors and there are in them four caracutes to be taxed and three churches"*. It is likely that the three churches were Bentham, Tunstall and Tatham. Dr. Whitaker [1801] says, *"Bentham Church, as it now appears, is a low plain uniform building of about the time of Henry VII, with tower, side aisles, clerestory, and tower, the column slender and angular."*

As the Saxon style of architecture prevailed from the close of the sixth century to the middle of the eleventh century one may reasonably conclude that the first church was a wooden structure, as most of the early churches were made of the trees cut down in the primeval forests. In the Saxon chronicle it is written that the first church or minster built by Eadwine at York was built of trees or wood. If the church at the Domesday Survey existed it was built some time before the Norman Conquest, and its architecture would be in accordance with that which prevailed from the middle of the eleventh century to the latter part of the twelfth century. At the time of my visit there was but one sample remaining of the Norman structure and it was a piscina, which still occupied its ancient place under the fenestella.

Whatever decision may be adopted as to the style of architecture before the church was rebuilt in 1823, it is sufficiently evident that the structure was of a very debased kind of English. No doubt the alterations, such as raising the side walls and the roof of the nave, and fixing up three side galleries were made with the best intentions to increase the sitting accommodation and comfort of the parishioners, still as far as church architecture was concerned it was far from effective. The narrow pews, with their lofty backs, the cumbersome and too highly elevated pulpit, and the uncouth horizontal galleries, did not well harmonise with what a church should be. Much has been said by the Bishop of the diocese, some clergymen and architects, against the lofty pulpit, but if it had not been thus elevated, such was the structure of the galleries that the hearers in that part of the church would have seen very little of the preacher.

The pews in the gallery were chiefly square ones of good dimensions, cushioned and lined with baize, carpeted and well supplied with hassocks, so that the occupants should comfortably join in the service or quietly dose during the sermon. These pews were considered a kind of private property, consequently the ordinary churchgoers never thought of going into the gallery. Mr. Johnson, Grove Hill, had one. Mr. Roughsedge had one of the principal pews, and as far as my memory serves me, he had his coat of arms fixed up in it. The pillars and some of the arches in the church and windows were much admired by persons who took an interest in ancient architecture. There was a neat low painted arch from the vestry into the chancel, and it was supposed that before the Reformation this was the priest's entrance from the churchyard to that part of the church.

On entering the south door to the church there was on the right side projecting from the east wall a stone of a lozenge shape with the letters I.B. standing out in bold relief. For a long time the letters puzzled antiquarians, but it is believed that they stood for John the Baptist, the patron saint of the Church. Where this stone projected there used to be a large pew called the christening pew. The font used at that time was like a druggist's mortar. Anciently this part of the Church was the baptistry. At the time of my visit the place was occupied with a beautiful font of Caen stone resting on four elegant circular granite pillars, the gift of Mr. Teale's family of The Ridding. The inscription at the base was "*Suffer little children, and forbid them not to come unto me, &c.*"

It was said by some of the oldest inhabitants that the old pews before the alterations were made in 1823 were large and open, with seats on two sides and thick oaken thresholds. The floors were earthen, and for the comfort of the

St. John the Baptist's Church, Low Bentham, rebuilt in 1822 and photographed immediately before its demolition in 1876.

worshippers they were covered with either straw or rushes. On the south side of the Church there were two doors, and the one near the tower had a porch with a stone seat on each side. The ancient porch was removed and the doorway made up. The space gained within the Church afforded room for a good-sized pew. Before the Church was rebuilt the roof on the north side came down so near the ground that a woman of ordinary stature could reach the eaves.

In olden times it was usual to beautify the exterior of village churches with rough casting. A matter of this kind is frequently referred to in the old Ingleton parochial book of 1721. Some Lancastrians had the charge of the alterations within the Church, and a tradesman of Lower Bentham named Bunting had that of rough casting the outside. While doing this work he met with an accident, which happily did not prove fatal. While suspended at his work through some mishap he was thrown to the ground. It was well the steeple was not interfered with during the alterations which were made in 1823, with the exception of an arched doorway on the west in place of the one which had been walled up on the south.

Before additional sitting room was made by the erection of the galleries the Sunday School boys from Higher Bentham used to sit in the bell loft where the ringers used to ring the bells. There are not many of them now living who can remember one of the bell-ringers being caught up as by magic, and when he reached the ceiling he came down again as quickly as he was drawn up. The square tower was considered an elegant and well proportioned piece of church architecture. On account of its massive and fine looking masonry the Liverpool Archaeological Society had it lithographed. All its pinnacles on its angles were more or less defaced. The pinnacle on the north east was broken off at its base. The views of the Wenning and the surrounding country from the tower were very fine. Though the site of the Church is not many feet above the level of the river, still the limited landscape of woods, lands, and water was very fine. From the steeple there was a fine view of Robert Hall, an ancient residence of the Cantsfields, but now of the Gerrards. Some years ago its domestic chapel was despoiled of its ecclesiastical fittings and converted into a barn.

The Rectory

The Rectory, a little on the south east of the Church, near the Wenning looked a substantial and good clergyman's house. Dr. Whitaker speaks of it as, "*A hall looking building, with a centre and two wings, and is indebted to its trefoil lights for a pleasing air of antiquity suited to the character of the piece*". The Rectory appeared from its inner construction to have been originally a place of very small dimensions, consisting of a refectory, a small cooking apartment, and a dormitory. Some of the old walls of the ancient structure were four feet in thickness. Many additions had been made to the original building and much was done during the rectorship of the Rev. E. Sherlock to improve the Rectory and to give it a neater appearance. The Rectory, garden, grounds, and outbuildings formed a very pleasant and commodious gentleman's residence.

Bill from the Lancaster Guardian charging Low Bentham P.C.C. 5/- for the advert which announced the Church reopening, together with the actual published entry below.

BENTHAM.

THE PARISH CHURCH
WILL (D.V.)
BE RE-OPENED
On SATURDAY, APRIL 27th, at 2·30 P.M.
Sermon by
THE RT. REV. THE LORD BISHOP OF RIPON.

THE Services and Sermons on Sunday the 28th will be :—
Morning at 10·30, Rev. F. W. Joy, M.A., Bury S. Edmunds.
Afternoon at 3·0, The Rev. The Rector of Bentham.
Evening at 6·30, Rev. T. D. Sherlock, Vicar of Ingleton.
The Offertories at all the Services will be devoted to the current expenses of the Church.   [802

Early Rectors

It may be of interest to the parishioners to know who were the rectors and incumbents of olden times. Most of the following names are taken from Torre's Archdeaconry of Richmond and a registry at Chester, as the parish was in that diocese until 1836:- A.D.1374, D'ns Edm. Mirescue; 20th July 1394, D'ns Nic. Otterburn; 20th Sept. 1421, D'ns Tho. Swetynge, Cap.; 1462, Robt Fishe, Cl., Thomas Leson; 1546, Richard Fielding; 8th July 1568, Anthony Hopkins; [*see footnote] 18th Nov. 1588, Robert Field; 29th May 1616, X'opher Featherstone, Cl, M.A.; 25th August 1660, Robert Lowther; 24th January 1670, Edward Fell, M.A.; 9th October 1693, Thomas Lupton; July 1717, Thomas Lupton; 17th June 1720, Richard Goodhall; 26th March 1743, James Cowgill; 3rd January 1748, Oliver Marton, B.A.; 26th November 1761, Edward Fell; 16th December 1761, Thomas Butler, B.A.; 3rd October 1825, John Fleming Parker; 20th January 1863, William Clayton, M.A.; 7th March 1865, Matthew Wood, M.A.; 22nd August 1865, Edgar Sherlock, M.A.

A sad affair took place in the Parish Church during the close of the Rev. Chr. Featherstone's long rectorship. In an appendix to the life of William and Alice Ellis it is said, *"About the year 1652 or 1653 it was ordered that some of the servants, messengers, and followers of Jesus Christ (their teacher) were drawn to visit a people at or near unto a town called Bentham, namely, William Dewsbury, Richard Farneworth, Robert Hall, and John Snayden. Now the aforesaid Robert Hall, having a concern upon him to visit the steeple-house at Bentham aforesaid, was sorely beaten and bruised, in such sort that he died a short time after."* No doubt friend Hall said some plain Gospel truths both to the clergyman and his congregation with the best intentions, but the people did not look at it in that light, and consequently the interruption ended tragically in a good man's death.

* The modern Church notice board also includes: 1582 Robert Fishe.]

THE LANCASTER GUARDIAN
ESTABLISHED 1837. PRICE 1d.

The *Guardian* is distinguished by the accuracy and fulness of its LOCAL REPORTS, by its complete record of DISTRICT INTELLIGENCE, and it seeks to keep its readers well informed on the POLITICAL, GENERAL, and LITERARY NEWS OF THE WEEK.

TO ADVERTISERS.—Having been established over 40 years, the *Guardian* has gained a very eminent position as a Family Newspaper and an influential medium for Advertisements Its circulation has now so largely increased in all directions, and amongst all classes, that it has been recognised as THE BEST ADVERTISER in North Lancashire, the adjoining districts of Westmorland and the West Riding of Yorkshire, and particularly in Lunesdale, Craven and Ribblesdale.

The *Guardian* is issued at an earlier hour on Friday, in order to permit its despatch by the afternoon trains, but subsequent editions will be issued when required by the arrival of Later News and Local Reports.

Guardian Office, Church Street, Lancaster.

No.6 (10th April, 1897)

Low Bentham Parish Church

The Rev. E. Sherlock, who very kindly gave me any information of interest, said that a few years ago when he was superintending the laying of the new floor within the Communion rails, some records of the dead were laid bare. The most interesting and eccentric was that of the Rev. C. Featherstone. On a brass plate inlaid in the stone covering the remains of the Rector were the following inscriptions in Latin and English, which were deciphered by Mr. Sherlock with some difficulty:-

> Conditur hac parva generosus Rector in urna
> Corpus terra tegit, spiritus astra colit,
> Pluma refert animam, sic saxum corporis umbram,
> Pluma volat, saxum nunc jacet hoc tumulo.
> Who list to know who lyes under this stone,
> Sometimes a man, but now is fled and gone,
> His soul like to a feather flyes aloft,
> His body stone like to his Centre soft,
> What I have been thou art; and thou shall be,
> What now I am, loe this is Destinie.

Christoferus Fetherstone artium Magister Rector Ecclesiae de Bentham incumbens, succumbens, Obiit Octobris 14 to anno 1653.

On another brass plate inlaid in the stone there was the following inscription:- "Here lies the bodies of Rev. Thomas Lupton, who was rector of this Church 6 and 50 years, and died February 3 anno domini 1758, in the 81st year of his age; and of Mrs. Mary Lupton, who died August 2nd, anno domini 1696, in the 56th year of her age." According to the above record, he was in his 19th year of age when his wife died, and that when they were married there was a difference of 37 years in their ages. The last corpses interred within the Communion rails were those of the wife and daughter of the Rev. Mr. Robinson, who succeeded the late Rev. Richard Skirrow in the curacy. Mrs. Robinson died December 2nd 1840, aged 31 years, and her daughter died November 10th the same year, aged 4 months.

At an early date, interments in Church were far too common, and no doubt that chiefly arose from the dues for the privilege being little more in excess of those for burial in the Churchyard. Over seventy years ago, in sultry summer weather, it was no unusual thing for persons to be taken out of the Church in a swoon or fainting fit, which was always attributed to the effluvium which emanated from the mouldering dead.

Through the kindness of Mr. Sherlock I was permitted to look over three small volumes of parchment, containing records of baptisms, marriages, and burials from 1673 to 1783. The registers to the close of 1719 were in Latin, and afterwards in English. When an illegitimate child was baptised its mother's name for shame was

St. John the Baptist's Church, Low Bentham. The rebuilt church was opened in 1878, with only the tower and part of the chancel remaining from its predecessor.

omitted. An instance will show how brief and plain the record was. *"Richard, a bastard child, baptised July ye 4 day, 1720."* This was punishing the lad for his mother's sin, and leaving an important record without a surname. A few extracts from the registers will not be without interest to some of the descendants of old Bentham families:

> Thomas and Elizabeth Wray, baptised August 4,1722.
> George Holden married by licence to Jane Brook, spinster, September 20th 1755.
> Christo Ellershaw et John Preston Sepulti erant, Feb.9th 1682.
> Jane Uxor Richardi Robinson Sepulti erat March 1689.
> Eliza Overend Vid Sepulta Sep.27 1689.
> George Holden departed this life 1793, and Jane his wife 1761.

There was a mural tablet in the church with a Latin inscription regarding the deaths of Mr. Holden and his wife. It was rather remarkable that there were so few mural tablets in the church. Amongst them there was one to the members of the Rev. T. Butler's family, one to John Townson, of Mewith Head, near Bentham, dated 1775; one to Agnes Garnett, Upper Bentham, and mother of the late Thomas Garnett, surgeon, Lancaster, and dated 1790; one to John Wilkinson, Higher Bentham, 1811.

One of a recent date was a memorial window to *"Alfred Foster, M.A. of Spring Head, Halifax, who died July 10th 1873. This window is placed by his friend Walker Joy, Easter 1874."* The window consisted of two lights, one representing the baptism of the Saviour and the other Christ's interview with Nicodemus. Beneath the one the spirit of God was moving upon the face of the waters, and beneath the other the Ark was floating on the waters. At the top of the figures there were angels with appropriate mottoes on a scroll. The window, which was a beautiful work of art, was by Hardman.

On the east side of the churchyard was an ancient headstone of a Knight Templar, on which there were many devices, but the inscription was illegible. On an oaken board in the belfry there were the following lines, *"Who ryngs thys belle, let hym take welle to hande, and hedde, and herte, ye hande for worke, ye hedde for wytte, ye herte for worshyppe."*

Rev. Thomas Wray

Since taking it in hand some notes, which have for many years been amongst my papers, relating to two of the most eminent characters, the Rev. Thomas Wray and the Rev. George Holden, have turned up. The first was a D.D. and fellow of Christ College, Cambridge. He was successively chaplain to Archbishops Hutton and Secker. He was born of poor and humble parents, and still by plodding perseverance at his books and studies he rose to great eminence in the Church of England. He was pious, abstemious and of great self control. He was of a weak constitution and was never married.

Though he was most amiable in his deportment, still he was a zealous reprover of vice in public and private. He learned from his master, Archbishop Secker, not to despise the meanest nor to shirk the most disagreeable offices of his function. He was Vicar of Rochdale where he died Feb. 22nd 1778, aged 56 years. A plain stone was erected to his memory within the altar rails.

Wray was not a common name either at Bentham or in the neighbourhood as it is not amongst the ancient names of Ewecross Division. In my early schoolboy days a Richard Ray in Mewith removed his business as grocer and provision dealer to Upper Bentham, and built his premises on the hill at the east side of the village. His house, which adjoined his shop, was named Mount Place. All the members of the family spelt their name Ray.

Rev. George Holden

The Rev. George Holden was one of the first masters at Collingwood Free Grammar School, Upper Bentham. The name is first mentioned in 1755, that was the year in which he married Jane Brook. At the time the Rev. Thomas Benson was the headmaster, and Mr. Holden was the second master. According to Mr. Collingwood's will the headmaster's salary was fixed at £30 a year and the second master's at £20. The second master was to have an addition of £5 for reading the prayers of the Church of England to twelve poor hospitallers. The niggardly salaries of those reverends were a little augmented by what was called the cockpenny which was due yearly on Pancake Tuesday.

Mr. Holden was the father of the Rev. George Holden, LL.D., who was parson and schoolmaster in the parish of Horton-in-Ribblesdale, where he died December 31st 1820. It is said that for nearly 40 years he was master of Horton Free Grammar School, and that during his mastership he educated a greater number of clergymen for the Episcopal Church of England than any classical teacher under similar circumstances. He was a man of high classical and mathematical attainments. He was eminent by the calculations of correct time tables which were of great service to Liverpool, and on this account they were published as "*Holden's Liverpool Tide Tables*". His mother (Jane Brook) belonged to an old Bentham family.

Rev. James Brook

In 1796 the Rev. Thomas Benson resigned the headmastership of Collingwood's Free Grammar School after fifty years service, and was succeeded by the Rev. James Brook, of the University College, Oxford. It is likely that this schoolmaster was Mrs. Holden's brother. On the 24th of February 1815, the Rev. James Brook died after holding the headmastership for twenty years.

When I was a boy there was a Parson Brook at Tatham Parish Church, who had one daughter who was the heir to the Brook's estate at Upper Bentham. Their family house adjoined the Skirrow's property, and for a long course of years was occupied by the late John Swainson. Parson Brook, in a reason of sickness, rose from his bed in the dark to take some medicine when he made a fatal mistake by taking it from a wrong bottle. A sister of his, Ann Croft, a captain's widow, lived in a house adjoining a barn on the west, opposite to the Quaker's Meeting House. Her daughter, Mrs. Downham, and family left Bentham fifty or sixty years ago, and they were the last of the Bentham Brook's family. Her last uncle, Clapham Brook, who was never married, I think, died before the Downham's left Bentham.

The Overend Family

One of them generally went by the name of Justice Overend. I have reason to believe that some of their members were not natives of Bentham. An old man of the name of John Scott, who was over 80 years of age when he died, told me many years ago that his grandfather, when he was a young man, came from some part of Lancashire with Justice Overend to Bentham. No doubt he was a manufacturer of calico, and that he put out weaving before Bentham Mill was built. In most of the neighbouring villages, especially Burton-in-Lonsdale, there was a deal of cotton weaving. Weaving in the cottages was common at the beginning of the 18th century.

There are many of Overend's tokens still in existence. Many years ago Mr. T. Brayshaw, of Settle, showed one he had had in his possession for some time. I have one in excellent preservation, about the size of a sixpence, which was given to me by Mr. J. T. Coates. It is beautifully ornamented, and on one side there is "*John Overend, O.F.*" in a circle. There is in an inner circle three figures like sheep. If so, they might be emblematical of a woollen business. On the other side, in a circle there is "*Bentham, 1666*" and two stars in the centre. In an inner circle there are "*L.O.*" and some stars. Mr. Speight, in "***Yorkshire Highlands***", speaks of one of them about the size of a sixpence, which bears on the obverse side the figure of a shuttle, with the words "*Will. Overend. In Bentham*", and on the reverse side is inscribed "*His Halfe Penny 1666*". In the centre there are the letters "*W.D.O.*" There are other tokens of later date, with similar inscriptions.

The Ellershaws

The Ellershaws at one time were yeoman of more than common importance in the parish, especially in connection with the Collingwood Trust. In 1732, John and Thomas Ellershaw were added to the trusteeship, and subsequently Henry and William Ellershaw. When I was a boy of five or six years of age there lived at the lower end of the village one Thomas Ellershaw, who lived on his means. He lived in an ancient house, with a good stone porch at the entrance, and it is now the third house on the east side of what was called 70 years ago Bedlam Row. It has been renamed Scotland Row. Much of the land from Scotland Row to the site on which the Wesleyan Chapel and School stands and land northward belonged to Thomas Ellershaw. There were lateral branches of the family, but the old name of Ellershaw has disappeared from Bentham more than sixty years ago. There was a family of the name of Ellershaw at Stone Gate, Lower Bentham, but the name passed out of the family nearly seventy years ago on the death of an only son, Christopher Ellershaw.

Low Bentham Church Rebuild

In 1877-8 the Church was restored under the management of Mr. Norman Shaw, R.A. As I have not had the privilege of visiting the new construction on a weekday, I cannot say much except on the information of others. Mr. Speight, in his book already referred to, says Mr. Shaw transformed ugliness into beauty, and disclosed many things of rare interest long hidden from view, while under the fostering care of the late Rector, the Rev. F. W. Joy, D.D., who is a Fellow of the Society of Antiquaries, a number of relics have been discovered and most tastefully restored. The style of architecture is perpendicular throughout, the old arches being exceedingly fine for proportion.

The beautiful east window by Powell of London is of five lights and illustrates the following Scriptural subjects:- The salutation, the naming of Jesus [sic: this should read John], the baptism of Christ, the reproving of Herod, and the martyrdom of John. A window on the south side of the chancel is to the memory of the late Mr. Joseph Teale, who died in 1889. The left hand light represents the angel of the Revelation (chapter xxii, 1 and 2), *"And he showed me a pure river of water clear as crystal, proceeding out of the throne of God and of the Lamb"*. The right hand light has for its subject the Angel going down to the pool of Bethseda and troubling the water (St. John, chapter 5, 2). There are other handsome memorial windows, viz., one to Mr. John Swainson and his wife Elizabeth Susannah Swainson of Halton Hall (erected 1878) and one to Mrs. Eleanor Burrow, who died in 1873, put in by her niece, Mary Alice Just, in 1886.

The Samaritan Sick Club

Many changes have taken place at the Church; all the old choirs have passed away, as well as the parsons, clerks, sextons, and most of the old Sunday scholars who attended the morning service from Upper Bentham, and the old Samaritan Sick Club, the anniversaries of which had been identified with the Parish Church for nearly seventy years. What a stir and excitement there used to be at early morn on the 23rd of June when the Club sticks and the fine old Samaritan flag had to be fetched from the large room at Bentham House, and everything had to be made ready for a long procession to St. John's Church. Who that witnessed the marshalling of the members and the pride with which the officers directed their movements in their march to the Parish Church can ever forget the pleasure that was universally manifested on the occasion.

The colour, as it was called, representing an eastern traveller on his way from Jerusalem to Jericho, stripped of his clothing, wounded and left half dead by robbers, and a priest passing by on one side and the Levite, while a good Samaritan pours into his wounds oil and wine, and his ass looks approvingly on, was a grand sight and a grand lesson to the lads and lasses of both Benthams, who delighted to see it wave in the breeze, *"Go thou and do likewise"*, in fine looking letters, pointing out to priest and people the lesson, always ready to do a kindness to him who needs it.

Now Ready, 3rd Edition, Revised and Corrected,
RAMBLES ABOUT INGLETON.
By J. CARR.
PRICE 3d.
At the *GUARDIAN* OFFICE.

No. 7 (17th April, 1897)

Nonconformist Churches

Happily Lower Bentham is not overdone with religious denominations like many small villages, and evidently they are striving to build one another up in the one faith that Jesus Christ is the foundation, sole, and supreme head of the Christian Church. That He is the mediator between God and men, and the ransom of the human race, and that their principal mission is to turn all men if possible from the error of their ways, and to bring them into the union of the spirit and to dwell in love and peace one with another.

The Friends Meeting, Calf Cop

In giving brief biographical notes, &c. of Nonconformists at Bentham, the Quakers or Friends, as to time have a prior claim. It is rather remarkable that the Friends prospered the most in their ministry when persecution and cruel penalties fell heavily upon them than in more peaceable times. It is an old saying, "*The blood of the martyrs is the seed of the Church*". This has been the case at all the meetings included in the Settle monthly meeting. In 1851, there were no members at Ilkley but there were seven attenders, at Airton there were seven members, and they were comprised in one family living on the Meeting House estate. At Newton-in-Bowland there were two members and seven attenders. Even at Skipton, where Friends used to be so numerous and influential, there were only three members and four attenders. One of the members who died recently was Robert Chester, who at one time worshipped with the Wesleyans at Bentham, and lived on a small farm at Fowgill.

The Rise of the Bentham Quakers

It is a question of whether there is any documentary evidence to show when Friends first made their appearance in the parish of Bentham. It is said, "*that about 1652 or 1653 when William Dewsbury, Richard Farneworth, Robert Hall, and John Snayden visited Bentham divers of the people were convinced of the truth, turned unto Christ, their teacher, on whom they often must together wait, &c. Their number since that time hath much increased so that now they have become a meeting of a considerable number of Friends, which is called Bentham Meeting.*". The old Meeting House at Calf Cop is dated 1718, which is 66 years after the Bentham Meeting was in existence. At the beginning of their Mission they frequently held their meetings at the houses of their friends as it was done at Settle in or about 1652 or 1653 when William Dewsbury first took his stand upon the Cross, when he was soon pulled down and much abused. A young man named John Armistead took him to his mothers where he was entertained. In the evening divers people were gathered to the house, unto whom he declaimed fervently against fruitless profession of religion, &c. It will be seen from the above date that the Bentham meeting is more ancient than that of Settle, for when William Dewsbury opened his ministry at Settle there was a considerable number of Friends called the Bentham Meeting. It is likely before the present meeting house was built there was one a little nearer Lower Bentham, where there is an old Quaker burial ground in a field on the left hand side of the road leading to the Calf Cop. A few years ago Mr. Thomas Barrow of Lancaster told me that a Friend who had been for some time in Lancaster Castle was under a severe sentence, one part of which was to have his tongue torn from his mouth to put a stop to his vocal ministry. He, through more merciful regulations, escaped his torture, and finally regained his liberty. At his death he found his resting place in the old burial ground referred to. Some of the old Bentham yeomen in George Foxs time were persecuted, heavily fined, and their cattle distrained and sold in the street at a great loss. If men had sense to learn that a mans religion was absolutely his God and himself there would be an end of persecution for both religious and political creeds.

The Dawn of Religious Liberty to the Society of Friends, &c.

When the Prince of Orange ascended the English throne he exerted himself with remarkable zeal to secure liberty of conscience in all matters relating to religious opinions and worship. He tried hard to abrogate the Act of Uniformity, the Conventicle Act, the Five Miles Act, the Test Act, and the other acts which harassed Dissenters. Though he could not accomplish all he wished he succeeded in getting the Toleration Act, called the Stat. 1. W. and M., 2c 18, which exempted on certain conditions the penalties of those unrepealed Acts. Those who wished to avail themselves of the benefits were required to subscribe 34 of the 39 articles of the Church of England, which most of the Protestant Dissenters could do. The Baptists were excused from professing belief in infant baptism and the Quakers from taking an oath if they professed a general belief in Christianity and promised fidelity to the Government and made a declaration against transubstantiation.

The Toleration Act, imperfect as it was, was a great benefit to Protestant Dissenters, and King William of glorious memory would have pushed religious liberty to its Bible limits, but he was bitterly opposed by a party who, if they had had the power, would have compelled all the nation to conformity to their creeds of religion and politics. *"Why"*, they said, *"have we denounced King James as a tyrant to bring in a man under the guise of a deliverer who, within ten weeks of his accession, has destroyed bulwarks of personal freedom which the discarded family (Stuarts) in their most arbitrary moments never once dared to touch."*

The Meeting house at Calf Cop was not built for twenty-nine years after the passing of the Toleration Act, so no doubt they had had previously another place of worship. Though the Toleration Act was intended to be a great relief to Dissenters, and especially to the Quakers, they had still to bear many expensive and galling exactions from the clergy. One instance may suffice, which is that of six Quakers who were prosecuted by a clergyman for Easter offerings to the amount of fourpence. This paltry sum in the Ecclesiastical Court was increased to £300. For this sum they were imprisoned, and if it had not been for their fellow-townsmen, by whom they were so highly esteemed that they subscribed the sum, they would not have been set free. A good idea may be formed of the times from the observations of his Lordship. He said that *"Subscribing the money would prove a ruinous kindness to the Quakers for it would wet the avarice of the clergy and proctors to such a degree that the people of that persuasion would everywhere be hunted down without mercy for small sums which might be recovered at once by the simple process of distraint."*

The Decline of Quakers at the Calf Cop Meeting

It is evident from the size of the Meeting House and its gallery that at one time there was a goodly number of members and attenders. It cannot be stated precisely when this decline first took place, but it is certain that the Bentham Meeting had fallen into small dimensions before the time of Charles Parker, one of the Lords of Ingleton Manor, and the Bentham Mill Company. He was a minister among the Friends, and his daughter (Miss Parker) and her governess and companion (Miss Wilson) taught a Sunday School, first at the old Grammar School, and afterwards at Bentham House, and a night school for mill girls. At this school sewing, &c., as well as reading and writing, were taught. On the first day Miss Parker and Miss Wilson used to conduct their scholars as far as the Parish Church gates, and then leave them to go to their meeting at Calf Cop. Chas. Parker, about 1817, removed from Bentham to Yealand, where he intended to spend his last days. He was very much respected by the mill hands and by the people of the two Benthams for his generosity and genial manners to rich and poor. When the High mill was burnt down, May 19th, 1803, he begged of the people not to risk their lives, as the loss of the mill was nothing to the loss of a life. He did all he could in finding the mill hands something to do while the mill was bring rebuilt. Though he built a beautiful family residence at Yealand, he did not enjoy it for many years. He died when on a visit in Suffolk July 6th, 1822, aged 72 years.

John Yeardly and Lairgill

Shortly after Charles Parker removed to Bentham John Yeardly, a noted minister, came to Bentham Mill. He says in a letter to his wife, dated 6mo. 23, 1817, *"H.R."* (meaning Hornby Roughsedge), *"if we should agree he wants me to go over directly to lay down plans for a few weavers houses, &c."* No doubt this refers to Lairgill Row, for many years known as Kirkham. I believe this row consists of seventeen houses to each of which there was a large cellar for sail cloth weaving. This was done when the Hornbys sailcloth weavers were about to be removed from Kirkham in Lancashire to Bentham. If not all the houses were occupied by Kirkham weavers a very large majority of them were and this was the reason why it was called Kirkham. Though I was only in my fifth year when they were built I remember a large number of men digging the foundations. On John Yeardlys coming to Bentham and uniting with the Bentham Meeting it was in a very low condition. In a letter to his wife he says, *"It is a very small meeting indeed, there are but two female Friends."* Those two Friends were Mary Townson and Grace Bellman, who withdrew from the Bentham Wesleyan Society in 1815. They kept the shop occupied by the late Mr. R. Wilcock, opposite the Black Bull in Upper Bentham. Grace Bellman for a long course of years was the only member of the Bentham Meeting who spoke at these meetings. She generally quoted a passage of Scripture, and then commented briefly on it in a homely and practical way. I remember being present on one occasion when she spoke and at the time there was not more than four or five persons present.

At the time John Yeardly was at Bentham there was one Jonathan Stordy, a Friend, who married one of the Cumberland family at Lower Bentham, and they were in connection with the Bentham Meeting. He removed to Penrith and entered into the ironmongery business, and died about 1845. Many years ago I met with Thomas Altham, his nephew, who still carried on the same business. I believe Cumberlands and Kendals were families at Lower Bentham, connected with the Friends and with each other by marriages. When I was a stripling of a lad John Kendal, a Friend, kept the shop which has been occupied for many years by members of the Holmes family, whence he removed to their own estate - Bracken Hill, near Calf Cop. Occasionally there were large meetings at the Meeting House, both above and below stairs were well filled and several even in the passage and in an adjoining room.

In 1820 John Yeardly says that after he had attended a quarterly meeting for worship that he was, *"favoured with more enlargement of love towards the members of his small meeting."* Having been long under a weighty impression that he had a call to exercise his ministry in foreign lands, in 1821 he decided to leave Bentham for that purpose. Before doing so he visited the grave of his recently deceased wife in the Friends burial ground. He says, *"This day 1821, 11 mo., 18, I visited, perhaps for the last time, the place which encloses the relics of one so dearly beloved, and as I stood weeping over her grave it sprang in my heart, She is not here, but she is risen. What an unspeakable consolation, to be enabled to leave the dust behind, and hold sweet communion and converse with the spirit."* John Yeardly in his ministry made five continental journeys, besides visiting Russia, Asiatic Turkey, &c., and was seized with paralysis near Constantinople, when he hastened to his house at Stamford Hill, where he arrived on the 9th of August, 1858, and died on the 11th, aged 72 years. He was buried at Stoke Newington, on the 18th.

The Revival of Quakerism at the Bentham Meeting

Mr. and Mrs. Rice took up their home at Upper Bentham about forty-five years ago, and as Friends they united with the Bentham meeting. The late Christopher Knowles also united with the Friends, and, with John Thomas Rice, did much to extend the Quakers interest in the two Benthams. Mr. Rice, having means and influence, took much interest in promoting the revival. He, his wife, and Christopher Knowles were recorded and authorised ministers of the Bentham Meeting. Mr. Rice employed, at various times, a kind of missionary or schoolmaster, &c. William A. Pope and John W. Kaye carried on a school in the Wesleyan Schoolroom. They also made themselves useful in the temperance movement, and in matters connected with the Bentham Meeting. William A. Pope, on leaving Bentham, joined the Unitarians, and became one of their ministers. On spending a holiday in Cumberland he met with a fatal accident. He was ardently fond of mountain climbing, and while so doing he took a spring from one crag to another, when he overbalanced himself and fell over a precipice. John W. Kaye on leaving Bentham, became a minister of the Church of England, and settled in Ireland. The next two engaged were not so much employed in religious matters as in things temporal. They were Septimus Davis and Moses Pullen. Still they were connected with the Bentham Meeting. Moses Pullen died a few months ago in the neighbourhood of Birmingham. Septimus Davis went to the United States and settled down as a farmer. Joseph John Dymond, a ministering Friend of Bradford, when crossing the American continent on a stage coach, in Ohio, homeward, said to the driver, "*That person who is coming towards us is like a man I have seen in Bentham.*" On meeting the pedestrian he threw up his arms and exclaimed, "*Who would have expected to meet Joseph John Dymond half across America?*"

Popular Measures for an Extending the Revival

In 1864 a meeting house was built in Upper Bentham and school rooms, after which a Sunday school was opened which was quite a new thing amongst the Quakers. In addition to this there was a bible reading for adults, shortly before morning worship. As there was no service in the evening of First Day a meeting was held in a public room, where the bible was read with short comments, and then the meeting was opened to anyone who felt that he had a word in season to say to the people. Being at the meeting on one occasion Mr. Rice said that if I felt a desire to speak there was freedom of speech. An old ministering friend, whose labours are ended, said to me, "*We have a free platform for anyone who is a true disciple of Christ.*" These additional means to what is spoken of as worship were quite a success. The first day school is still carried on, but the bible meetings are discontinued. When Mr. Rice died, in 1872, it was a serious loss to Bentham Meeting. There was great lamentation over the loss, and at his funeral there was an overwhelming attendance. There were many leading Friends present, and the occasion as a religious service was solemn and weighty. The statistics of 1881 show that great progress had been made, and that the Bentham meeting stood well in the Brighouse monthly meeting. At this date there were 48 members and 61 attenders. This was much higher than Settle with its 23 members and 20 attenders. In the Brighouse list of seventeen Particular Meetings, Bentham occupied the fifth place, and those that headed the list were Leeds, Bradford, Huddersfield, and Halifax. A few years after Mr. Rice's decease Mrs. Rice left Bentham and the Bentham meeting. Her heart was in the work he had undertaken and she was never behind in any good work either of a religious or temporal character that was for the good of the community. The more recent loss to the Bentham meeting was the late Christopher Knowles, whose heart was warm in any good work for the furtherance of peace, temperance, religious and political freedom. With all the removals and deaths referred to the Bentham meeting more than maintains its ground for at the present time it numbers 60 members beside attenders.

No.8 (24th April, 1897)

The Introduction of Methodism into Lower Bentham

It took a long series of years and many futile attempts to establish a Methodist Church in the village. Three reasons may account for this long delay, one of which was, there was a neat little chapel opened in the upper village in 1820. At this date people did not think much at going a mile or two to Bentham Chapel. In my youth I remember people coming from Upper Greystonegill, from Lowgill, and near Guy Hill in Tatham. Another reason was the people in Lower Bentham were not favourable to Methodism, and a very large majority of them looked upon it as an encroachment on the Church of England. They considered the Methodists a low class of people somewhat deranged in their minds. They, by some of the inhabitants, were denounced as fanatics or people beside themselves. Even some of the working-class considered it a disgrace to be identified with them. A considerable number of years ago I was well acquainted with a family who had a deeply-rooted antipathy to anything of a Methodistical character. They had but one child (a son), who, when he arrived at a proper age, was apprenticed to a master at a distant town where the Methodist body was pretty strong. He was a fine young man, a credit to himself and his parents, but when his father and mother heard of his conversion and his having joined the Methodists, they felt so deeply wounded that they wept over the disgrace. They made no secret of it and told some of their friends that never such a disgrace had fallen on their family before. The young man, who, during his connection with the Wesleyans, conducted himself with becoming Christian propriety, unhappily died just when he was likely for becoming a useful member of the church of his choice. His parents, who were fairly advanced in life, did not long survive him, and with their death the family line became extinct. Perhaps the chief reason why Methodism was retarded was a want of that sturdy perseverance which was so common in the early days of Methodism in breaking up fresh ground.

The First Attempt to Introduce Methodism

If any efforts had been made previously it was not within my recollection, and I never heard of them. About 1833 a young man of the name of Robinson and some other friends began religious services on a Sunday evening at 5 p.m., in a room near to where Eller beck enters the village. The meetings were pretty well attended for a time, but as Robinson was young and inexperienced it was not possible for him to keep up the interest without additional help. The Rev. Mr. Darnley, the only circuit minister, had too much on hand to attend to this new movement. In consequence of this lack of labourers the congregations soon dwindled down to small dimensions, and eventually the room was closed. Many years passed away before any further attempt was made to establish a Methodist cause. In 1837 or 8, as I had had some training in the Lancaster circuit in open services, in the summer season I frequently held meetings on the Sunday evening in the street. On leaving England for France in 1839 these services were not continued by the Upper Bentham local preachers.

The Second Attempt to get a Footing in the Village

Between fifty and sixty years ago George Phillipson, a member of an old Upper Bentham Wesleyan family, and Charles Wright, a local preacher, settled at Lower Bentham. They decided to make an effort to open preaching in a cottage and to form a Sunday School. At this time there were two preachers in Settle circuit, and the Rev. Mr. Stokes, the second preacher, lived in the upper village. The class consisted of five members, the leader of which was William Townson, and the class was held in George Phillipson's house. The Sunday School was held at the house of the late Mrs. Balderston. As all the men who started the first Wesleyan Sunday School, &c., in the village have been dead for very many years, it will not be unseemly to give their names. George Phillipson, Hugh McMahon, William Walker, and John Armistead. When the cottage became too small for the school two cottages were taken at a place called the Lions Den. The preaching place was Mr. Hugh Armisteads barn at the upper end of the village called "*Crow Trees*".

Mr. Armistead generously offered the Wesleyans land free for a Chapel if they would accept it for that purpose. Instead of doing that Mr. Stokes discontinued the preaching, and the five members were powerless to do anything in the way of building unaided by the Church and other friends. The quarterly class money only amounted to five shillings, so Mr. Stokes did not think the cause was worthy of being sustained. No doubt this was an error on the part of Mr. Stokes, for this is not the way Methodism has been built up amongst the nations and races of mankind. Mr. Stokes had been a missionary in the Shetland Islands, and he was an earnest and serious preacher, and his labours were much valued in Settle circuit. The five men were working men with scanty wages, and the five shillings were given by two of them, and they felt it was as much as they could give. By this ministerial mistake Lower Bentham was again closed against Methodism. Mr. Hugh Armistead, who was a retired farmer and of an old Methodist family, lived all his farming days at Robert Hall, and his father before him. When what is now the Settle Circuit was included in the Lancaster Circuit, there were only two travelling preachers, both of whom were stationed at Lancaster. For the Settle portion of the Circuit a horse was kept and the preachers alternately spent a fortnight at the Bentham and Settle end of the Circuit and when the preacher was planned at Bentham his horse was put up at Robert Hall free of expense. The father of the late Hugh Armistead remembered the Circuit horse in his will, and according to that descendant, it was to have free quarters at Robert Hall as long as it was occupied by a member of his family.

A New Start to Establish a Methodist Church in the Village

In 1881 the Rev. E. E. Thies was appointed the second preacher in the Settle Circuit, and was stationed at Upper Bentham. In 1882 or 1883 he began week-night preaching at Lower Bentham, and Mr. Alderman Ford kindly granted the Mill dining-room for the services. A class was also formed, and it met for some years at the house of the late Mr. Umpleby. Shortly after this auspicious beginning Sunday services were begun, and they were regularly supplied by the Circuit and lay preachers, and as a matter of course Lower Bentham took its place on the Circuit plan. The harness-room at Lake House, long the residence of the late Dr. Elletson was used as a place of worship. I remember officiating once or more in this rather singular and out of the way place of worship. In course of time the leaders of the cause, after the old Methodist custom, planned a series of revival services, and the late Mr. James McClellan, a local preacher in the Skipton Circuit, was engaged for the occasion. James McClellan, who was an excellent and zealous local preacher, stood high both in Settle and Skipton Circuits, and wherever he laboured his evangelical services were much appreciated.

The cause of Methodism had been so successful that in 1885 the Society and their friends considered that the time had come for them to build a new chapel. After prudent consideration as to how the money should be raised to carry out the scheme, Messrs. Whitaker, Umpleby, and J. Cumberland were appointed to receive subscriptions towards the building fund. It was said that, though the Lower Bentham friends were not rich, they had a mind to work. Such progress was made in the undertaking that it was decided to lay the foundation stones of this new Chapel on January 2nd, 1886. Many Wesleyans and friends met on the occasion, and, after suitable hymns had been sung and prayers offered for the success of the scheme and the divine protection of the building during the erection of the house of prayer, the ceremony usual on such occasions was carried out. The Church Ministers, the Revs. J. Harris and W. C. Kendal, and the Rev. J. W. Burns (a visitor), officiated on the occasion. The service throughout was of a most interesting character, and the assembled people evidently enjoyed the good things which had been spoken. As it would have been out of harmony with modern Methodism if the demonstration had not been followed with a good tea, Miss Leeming, an efficient caterer for the public, supplied a variety of good things to about one hundred guests. The money collected on the occasion was over £21.

The Opening of the New Chapel

This memorable event took place on the 3rd of July, 1886, when the day, for warmth and bright sunshine, was everything that could have been wished. If the first pioneers of Methodism in the village could have witnessed the event, they would have seen that their labours, though apparently futile, had not been entirely in vain. From the first attempt to introduce Methodism into the village to the opening of the chapel was fifty-three years. That was a long time before the Upper Bentham Wesleyans and the Settle Circuit entered heartily into the evangelical work of the five members who were deserted in the time of the Rev. Mr. Stokes. The preacher for the occasion was the Rev. E. R. Edwards, of Manningham, a popular minister, well known in the circuit. The text was taken from the 13th chapter of the First of Corinthians - *"When I was a child I thought as a child, I spoke as a child, I understood as a child, but when I became a man I put away childish things."* The sermon, which was highly instructive and promolative of consistent Christian conduct, was much appreciated. An adjournment was made to a barn, which was shortly crowded, for tea, where Miss Leeming had prepared an excellent and substantial spread, in the serving of which she was assisted by several of the ladies of the congregation.

There was an overflow meeting in the evening, when the Rev. W. C. Kendal, who occupied the chair, in a few brief remarks, congratulated the Lower Bentham Society and the Settle Circuit generally on the opening of the new chapel. It was a neat and well built house of prayer, an ornament to the village, and he hoped it would be of great service both to the congregation and the children who would attend the Sunday school. The chairman then called on Mr. Richard Sanderson to make the financial statement, which was as follows:- *"The expected cost of the chapel, with fittings. would be £380, and towards that sum £230 had been given and promised, so that £150 had still to be raised to pay off the remaining debt"*. The following gentlemen took part in the meeting:- the Rev. J. A. Barnes, of Headingley College, and Messrs. J. Bateson, Burton-in-Lonsdale, the late N. Saul, Upper Bentham, R.Camm, Clapham, and - Oldfield. Included amongst the votes of thanks one was given to Miss Leeming for the great help she had given to the building fund by her two or three teas, and to Grace Parker, who had collected money for a handsome pulpit, bible and a hymn book.

On the following day, the 4th of July, Mr. Barnes preached two excellent sermons to good congregations; the Rev. Mr. Cadman preached on the 11th; and the Rev. E. E. Thies on the 18th, all of which services were good and of a profitable character. At the close of these services the debt of £150 was reduced to £120. The gracious effects of the above opening services at once resulted in a wonderful accession to the cause. Fifty-seven seats were taken and a Sunday school was opened with fifty children. The Chapel, which will seat with comfort 150 people, is situated nearly in the centre of the village on the north. On the south side adjoining is a nice vestry suitable for class and other private meetings.

Further Progress of the Methodist Church

It used to be common for Methodists when they built chapels to involve the trustees in such heavy debt that it took more than a generation to liquidate it but now there is a more general disposition to free them from that encumbrance as quickly as possible. The friends of the church to cast off their burden arranged for a bazaar to take place on Friday and Saturday, the 27th and 28th of May 1887, and they secured the services of Mr. Benson Ford to open it. There was a large assortment of useful and fancy goods, and a goodly number of friends from different parts of the circuit were present to give a helping hand to reduce the chapel debt. After Mr. and Mrs. Ford made their appearance the proceedings began with the hymn, *"O, for a thousand tongues to sing"*, at the close of which the Rev. G. Dyer, the superintendent of the circuit, offered prayer. The Rev. J. Jackson called on Mr. Ford to open the bazaar, who in a brief speech full of good wishes spoke of the pleasure it afforded him and his wife to be present on the occasion. Happily Mr. Ford is one of those Friends whose catholicity in religious sentiment ever leads him to give his services to any cause for the uplifting of mankind and the promoting of every work for the moral and spiritual good of his fellow men. As a matter of courtesy a vote of thanks was given to Mr. and Mrs. Ford for their kindness in being present, after which the ladies at the stalls carried on a successful trade. Mr. Dyer said the debt was £207, and it was hoped it would be reduced by £100. The net proceeds of the bazaar was £78 1s. 4d., and this was supplemented by £51 15s. 6d. as donations, making a total of £129 16s. 10d. The money raised secured a connexional grant of £57 10s. At the present time the membership of the church is 40 members, and in the Sunday school there are 18 teachers and 90 scholars.

G. W. GARLICK,
TAILOR AND DRAPER,
NEW GOODS for the Present Season to hand to
WORSTRDS, SERGES, VICUNAS, SCOTCH
and WEST of ENGLAND SUITINGS.
READY-MADE SUITS in Boys', Youths' and Men's.

A Choice Assortment in all the Latest Styles in
DRESS GOODS, SATERNS, PRINTS,
CAPES, MANTLES & JACKETS.
INSPECTION INVITED.
An APPRENTICE WANTED. (162

No.9 (1st May, 1897)

The Primitive Methodists came into the Settle Circuit towards the end of the ministry of the Rev. Able Darnley, whose removal to the Appleby Circuit took place at the Conference of 1835. He felt somewhat grieved at this intrusion into his circuit, and I remember that he made the following remark that they had followed him into other circuits. It was not because he had any unchristian feelings against them, but the fact that it was calculated to cause separations from the Wesleyans, and to multiply sects in small villages. All the towns in Settle Circuit were small, with the exception of Settle, and he thought, like other sensible people, that to form two or three small Methodist societies in a small village was a waste of money and labour, which might be more usefully devoted where the Wesleyans had no field of labour. Nonconformist churches in recent years have seen the folly in this, and have suggested plans for not interfering with one another in small rural villages. Think of a small village having in it the Wesleyans, the Free Methodist Church, and the Primitives, when one chapel would hold more than the whole of the congregations, and especially when no one can perceive the slightest difference in their forms of worship and the doctrines their ministers preached. Certainly there is perfect freedom in matters of religious opinion, but is it either wise or economical to thus waste their forces? If the several Methodist denominations shall ever agree to form themselves into one church it will be a memorable era in their history and the world.

The Men Who First Introduced Primitive Methodism

Settle was the head of this mission and though it was not called a circuit, it included, in addition to Settle, Langcliffe, Low Bentham, Train Houses, High

Bentham, Ingleton, Proctors Row, Locks, West Side House, Newby, Giggleswick and Long Preston. The superintendent of this mission was the Rev. Mr. Langham, but at the time of his coming, the title of reverend was comparatively seldom used and evidently neither the minister nor the members cared for it. Mr. Langham was a sound and earnest gospel preacher and in every way qualified for an open air mission. He was fearless as an open air preacher and it did not need a choir to draw a congregation. He had a good musical voice, which he knew how to use to advantage. He had been many years engaged in mission work and, when he began his open air mission at Bentham it was evident that his work was telling on his naturally strong constitution. Shortly after the commencement of the mission, a young local preacher of the name of Jones was sent to assist Mr. Langham. He was sent under the auspices of a Primitive Methodist society at Huddersfield or in the neighbourhood, who guaranteed his salary. As they had undertaken this responsibility, they requested that Mr. Jones on his way to Settle should give them a call and preach a sermon to them, that they might judge as to whether he was suitable for the mission. When the youth made his appearance before the congregation, he felt somewhat depressed with a fear that he would break down. The preliminary part of the service passed off without a hitch, and a favourable impression was made. He had not gone far in his sermon, however, before he became so confused and incoherent that he broke down and was convulsed with tears. He sat down, and exclaimed, "*Glory be to God, I will go home.*" The church and congregation showed much sympathy for him, for they had seen and heard enough to show that the breakdown was not for lack of ability. The young man was encouraged and went on his journey with the prayers and good wishes of the people. Such a weeping breakdown was a good lesson at the start of the beginning of his wider ministry. Mr. Jones had not been long in the mission before his popularity began to gather large crowds at summer camp meetings and other open-air services.

The first time that I heard him was at a camp meeting at Hayburn, near Bentham. It was a brilliant summer day, and there was a large gathering of Primitives, Wesleyans, Church people, and persons who were not frequently seen at any place of worship. The young man was a charming speaker for an open-air service. The good old doctrines of the early Methodists were plainly and forcibly taught and impressed upon the people with good effect. The preacher's earnestness and emotional appeals to old and young had a surprising effect on his hearers. He was not a preacher who had trained himself to shed tears at stated intervals in his address, but a preacher who could make his hearers shed them while his own were held under proper restraint. It is a pleasure to me, after a space of about sixty years, to recall the cheering effect the meeting had on old Richard Hornby and his wife, who occupied the cottage on the farm. It was at this camp meeting I first became acquainted with my friend the late Christopher Knowles. It is very regrettable that the old-fashioned camp meetings and love feasts have nearly gone out of date.

The Primitive Cause at Lower Bentham

Though there was occasional preaching in the upper village it was at the lower end where the chief workers lived. As the five Wesleyan members who were deserted by the Rev. Mr. Stokes were in perfect harmony with the Primitives in doctrine and Christian experience, it was natural for them to join them in worship and Christian labour. The late Hugh McMahon opened his house for preaching, and John Clark opened his house for a Sunday School. About 1860 the Primitive Methodists had made considerable progress, and to carry on the ministry and Sunday School they contemplated building a chapel. As the Wesleyans had declined the offer of a free site for a new chapel from Mr. Hugh Armistead, the Primitives made application for the land, which was refused. Though Mr. Armistead did not grant the favour it would not be just to conclude that it arose from a split of opposition to the Primitives. He had been reared in an old Wesleyan family from his childhood, and he did not believe in encouraging divisions in the old body. At the time already mentioned there were regular Sunday and week night services, and the following had their names on the Settle Mission plan: A. Davies and W. Walker, local preachers, and Hugh McMahon and W. Phillipson, exhorters. Sometime after this date Robert Shuttleworth, Joshua Banks, W. Benn, and W. Ibbotson appeared on the plan as local preachers. Eight lay preachers in a small village like Lower Bentham was no mean staff of evangelists, and it was an evident sign of prosperity.

The members of this society paid special attention to the upper village and rendered needful help in their services held in cottages. Meetings were held in a cottage in Bedlam row and in the Square. I also remember attending some meetings in a cottage in the Hall Fold before the late Mr. Paul Pattinson purchased the property adjoining it. At that time there were two cottages and the Hall within the enclosure. The following neighbouring stations were on the plan: High Bentham, Ingleton, Ingleton Fells, and Newby-cum-Clapham. In 1850, according to the plan, none of the local preachers had any appointments at the above except Newby and Lower Bentham. The Rev. D. Kent, superintendent, preached once a fortnight on week nights at the upper village, and the same at Ingleton. Eventually for some time the Primitives secured the dancing room of the Kings Arms Inn for Sunday services.

The Building of a New Chapel

To unite the members and congregations of the two Benthams it was decided to build it somewhere between the two villages. It was finally decided to erect it on a site at a short distance on the west of the upper village on the left side of the road leading to the lower village. Some of the leading members thought that the Chapel would serve both villages, and that there was a more favourable prospect of success at the upper village. Some of the leading Friends and Wesleyans were not backward in giving them a helping hand on special occasions. I was present on one occasion at a missionary meeting, when Mr. Rice occupied the chair, and Mr. Constantine was one of the speakers. At this meeting it was evident that Primitive Methodism was not in a flourishing condition. When the Primitives first made their appearance in the neighbourhood they were generally spoken of as Ranters, and some of them took offence at what they considered an odious name. At that time my name was on their preachers plan, and I sometimes was called a Ranter. Some persons used the name with no intention of giving any offence, whilst others used it as a term of contempt. I remember on one occasion, just before I entered Lower Bentham, meeting two men, when one of them within hearing said, "*Who is that man?*" and the other replied, "*He's a Ranter preacher.*" I don't think either of them had any ill in them, and I was quite pleased at being called a Ranter.

The Decline and Collapse of Primitive Methodism

The chief cause was the removal of both members and a portion of the congregation to Lancaster, Manchester, Darlington, Barnoldswick, Nelson, &c. The last time I was planned at the Chapel, though it may be thirty years ago, will be long remembered. On my arrival at the Chapel there were neither members, Sunday School teachers, nor congregation. There were a few children playing in the road at their own sweet will. After waiting for some time without the arrival of teachers or congregation, I made for Ingleton by Robin Lane, and seeing the Roman Catholics enter their Chapel, I decided to follow them. The priest gave a nice and profitable address on the observance of the Sabbath Day, with which I was well pleased. At about the middle of the discourse the priest pulled out his snuffbox and took out a good pinch of snuff and snuffed with such force that it was evident that the lower portion of the nerves of the nostrils had been deadened by the habit. I had seen Scotchman hand their snuffboxes to one another in a place of worship, but I had never before seen it taken by a priest or a clergyman. Shortly after this last visit to the Primitive Methodist Chapel it was closed and eventually it was sold and made into a dwelling-house.

If the Cause Collapsed the Good Done Continued

As I was for many years acquainted with the Bentham local preachers and many of the members, I can bear witness that they were true to their Christian professions. William Walker, I knew from a child, and remember well when he and his brother were deserted in their infancy by a cruel father and thrown upon their mother, who had to work at the Mill for their maintenance. When old enough he was apprenticed to a flax-dresser. I have heard him tell how he and other young men, after their monthly pay-day, used to go into the fields to have a carousal of rum and new milk. He became an earnest and useful leader and local preacher, and some of his sons are following in his steps. After his removal to Colne I frequently met with him. On the last occasion he was the Baptist Chapel-keeper. (See footnote to article 10 in this series.)

Robert Shuttleworth was a rough sort of a youth, who had scarcely any schooling, and still a wonderful change took place in his manners, conversation and life under the Primitive Methodist ministry. He became a useful local preacher and quite a revivalist. He used to say he did enjoy a good shout at a meeting. Dont suppose he was a fool, as some one would have accounted him for using such an expression. Robert had the rest of the matter within him, and his daily life and

Sunday labour proved it. After Primitive Methodism collapsed, he joined the Wesleyans, amongst whom he is still a useful and laborious local preacher. He has a wide field for his ministry, as he is ever ready to serve the Free Methodist Church, the Primitives, or any other church where his services are required. To talk of Christianity being effete when it produces such fruits in a mans life and character is a mark of gross ignorance of the power of the gospel. Considering that Robert Shuttleworth was a raw and uncultured youth when he first became acquainted with the Primitives, I have marvelled at the wonderful elevating power the gospel has in refining and moulding the human character.

Ann Davies, a native of Upper Bentham, who was bereaved of her mother when a mere child, and thus debarred from such schooling as her help was much needed in her home, managed to triumph over great difficulties, and became a much respected and useful evangelist. She was a woman of good natural abilities, and she was soon pushed into the local ministry. She, with friends, visited the neighbouring villages, and with open air services did much useful work. I had initially known her from her birth, and seen her grow up to young womanhood, and naturally wished to hear her preach. I was astonished with her command of language and her correct speech, knowing that in her everyday life she had only been familiar with the Yorkshire dialect, which was spoken in the villages by a very large majority of the inhabitants. For many years she was a favourite evangelist and was engaged in revival meetings. Even after her marriage to the late Stephen Hall, a noble specimen of a man and a local preacher, she was called to distant places to conduct special services. Though now advanced in years she still holds fast the truth which in her youth made her free indeed.

William Bean was a noble example of the Gospel of Christ being the power of God unto salvation. The love of drink was his besetting sin, and I often noticed his movements when under its influence. He had a hard fight with his bodily and mental foe, and he never conquered until he fell into the hands of the Primitives. He, like brother Shuttleworth, gloried in a good shout. He removed to Lancaster with his father-in-law, James Smith, and family, and many of them joined the Lancaster Primitives. Since he removed to Lancaster I heard him on one occasion preach in the open air on the open space between the top of Penny Street and King Street. One Sunday forenoon, when going down the main street of Upper Bentham, William, who had come over on a visit, was holding an open air service on the ground on the west of the Poor-house. He made his voice heard to a considerable distance, and I was pleased to hear him, though I was not a shouter. When one knew his antecedents and the marvellous change which he had undergone, one could bear with his shouting. Joshua Banks, a man of a milder mould, removed to Nelson, where he still makes himself useful in the local ministry; he was a leader in the Lower Bentham Primitive body, and an acceptable preacher.

Droll Experiences of Some of the First Preachers

In some of the out-stations the poor people could not afford them comfort either in board or lodgings. A red herring, dry bread and a cup of tea for supper, and two chairs to lie on for a bed, were accepted without complaint. Turning sinners from the error of their ways was far from pleasant. A young man of the name of Braithwaite, who was as void of the appearance of a parson as it was possible to be, had manners as homely as his appearance. He was an excellent preacher and worker. His experience stands in contrast with the entertainment accorded to ministers of the present day. On sitting down to a cup of tea at the house of a lady farmer who did not drink tea, he complained of its nasty taste, when she said it was only fancy. He asked her to taste. Having done so, she looked into the cream jug to see whether anything was wrong there, when light dawned upon her memory, and she exclaimed, "*I made a cow drink in the kettle and forgot to wash it out.*" On another occasion he stayed with a farmer who, Irish fashion, allowed his geese to hatch their eggs in one of the bedrooms, so that he was angrily hissed at going to bed. Many other of his experiences were equally droll, which he bore with uncomplaining good humour. He was sent to a mission in Australia, but his young life was of short duration.

The Lancaster Guardian.
AND GENERAL ADVERTISER FOR THE NORTHERN COUNTIES
"GIVE ME THE LIBERTY TO KNOW, TO UTTER, AND TO ARGUE FREELY, ACCORDING TO CONSCIENCE."—*Milton.*

No.10 (8th May, 1897)

Cumberland and Marshall Families

It may readily be concluded that great improvements have been made in the local trades of the village since the beginning of the reign of Queen Victoria, and that the tradesmen of the present day are more pushing in business matters than their long past predecessors. It is somewhat remarkable that when the names of the past generations of tradesmen are compared with those of the present day, that there are only two names, Cumberland and Marshall, which were on the roll of tradesmen in 1822. Amongst the leading tradesmen of today are Cumberland Bros., builders, and Cumberland and Holmes, joiners. Cumberland is a very old Bentham family name, an ancient branch of which lived at Upper Bentham. The house and farm buildings which they occupied are still in good repair, and they stand on the south side of the street opposite the Wesleyan Sunday School. This was their home when Mr. Collingwood, the founder of the Grammar School and hospital for six widowers and the like number of widows, used to visit them. Mr. Collingwoods will was proved on January 20th, 1727, and the trustees of the charity were Messrs. Robert and John Cumberland and the Rev. R. Goodhall, the Rector of Bentham. Cumberland is the name that frequently occurs in the old marriage and funeral registers of the Parish Church.

Marshall is a name which has long been connected with the village, but most of the descendants are either dead or have moved to other places. Richard Marshall, the father of the present Richard, gardener, florist, &c., has been referred to as the originator of the Sandy Hill public gardens. He was far advanced in life when he married, and no doubt it was through his sister dying, who had been his faithful housekeeper for a long course of years. He found a suitable wife, a tidy and managing wife, in a housekeeper at the Rectory. He, considering his position, was a notability in many things, especially as a florist, horticulturist, and in other things. I became acquainted with him in my early teens, when he asked me to go with him one Sunday afternoon to Clapham to see the specially fine auriculas of a cousin of the name of Marshall. He made persevering efforts to open some of the coal beds in the parish, which on account their thinness did not yield much profit. He was a very homely man, and it was no mean pleasure to have an hours chat with him. He passed away at a good old age, I believe eighty years or more, and it is pleasant to revive those recollections of an old villager who was highly esteemed by his friends and neighbours.

Village Tradesmen

Mr. Thomas B. Boyd, tailor and postmaster, occupies a marked position amongst the tradesmen. A post office in a village is a much busier place now than it used to be in the middle of the present century. It was quite amusing to me a few years ago when travelling by the small gig in Ireland to see most of the country post offices crowded with policemen and others who were waiting for the mail! Mr. Boyd is a native of our village. I am well acquainted with the family and remember his old grandparents, Hugh Boyd and his wife. Though he has left our romantic neighbourhood, some of us who knew him in his boyhood are glad to know that he occupies so important a position in the village of his adoption. An official who comes daily in contact with people of every class may win golden opinions by his impartiality, urbanity, and readiness to please.

Mr. Thomas Hodkinson, draper, though he has been for many years a tradesman of the lower village, is a native of the upper village. On his mothers side he is a branch of the old Stephenson family of Upper Bentham. In 1832 the smallpox was very bad in the village and in the neighbourhood, when Mr. Hodkinsons father, I, and a young man of the name of Vipond escaped until it was dying out. We were the last sufferers, and all of us had a narrow escape, and I was presumed dead, and it was some time before a revival took place. This is the reason why the name Hodkinson is so deeply impressed on my mind. To show how careless the inhabitants of that day were in separating the affected from the healthy, the following instance may be mentioned. Children of both the healthy and the sick were allowed to sleep together from a notion that if they were foreordained to take the illness they would take it and vice versa. In one family there were seven boys and girls, and five or six of them were down at once with the disease, yet with their parents they all slept in one room. Under such circumstances it was marvellous that they all recovered.

Mr. Francis Bailey, coal dealer. I remember no Bailey amongst the village tradesmen, only the late James Bailey, joiner, and it may be that Mr. Francis is one of the family. The Baileys were the only joiners in the upper village when I was a boy, and they carried on business in an old thatched barn which stood with its gable ends north and south, on the site of which Mr. Gorrill some years ago built a house and shop. In course of time the roof fell, when John the joiner removed to a shippon and a barn which stood in a similar position, and it occupied the site of the house and shop built by Mr. Robert Jackson and in the possession of Mrs. Bentham. James Bailey removed to Lower Bentham and occupied a shop at the entrance of the village which is now the site of the Co-operative stores.

Misses Dodgson, milliners and dressmakers, are, I believe, a branch of the family of Jeremiah Dodgson, a notable man, whom I knew well in my early boyhood, and some of his sons, who for some years have been numbered amongst the departed. He was rather eccentric when slightly under the influence of drink, but even then he was a remarkably quiet man. He was a noted land measurer, and was spoken of as one of the best scholars in the district, and one that was well up in astronomy.

John Holmes, shoemaker and butter dealer, is a native of the lower village, but his father was a member of an old Upper Bentham family. Brian Holmes, of Lairgill Farm, at the east end of the village, was one of the old men in my school boy days. His son Brian, the youngest of his sons, who was some years older than I was, was one of the most active young men of the village. He was exceedingly fond of all the outdoor games which were common in his youth, and was skilful in them. His apprenticeship to the shoemaking business marked its decline in the neighbourhood. He was under the training of the late John Leak, who owned the premises now occupied by Mr. Seed, cabinetmaker, and the large shop was on the west. Most of the shoemakers in the district were trained in Leaks shop. The shop was not only noted at one time for its local trade, but for its connection with Clitheroe and other Lancashire towns, and even with foreign parts.

The late Brian Holmes and Richard Marsden were about the two last apprentices who served their time in the shop. The first opened a business at Lower Bentham, and the other at Langcliffe, near Settle. It was rather singular that two of the sons of Brian Holmes preferred the upper village to that of their nativity, and carried on successful businesses - Francis that of a tinman, painter, plumber, &c., and his brother that of a grocer, druggist, &c. Francis built a house and shop near the Midland Station, where he carried on business until his death. I was pretty well acquainted with him, as he occasionally worked for me. I esteemed him chiefly for his Christian and manly character. As a defender of Christianity in the local papers he did not hesitate to use plain and forcible language, and to append his name to what he had written. He was a noble lay helper and a good and faithful worker in connection with the village Church. His brother, who occupied the shop nearly opposite the shop of Knowles and Brothers, was connected with the Bentham Meeting of Friends, and one who gave the right hand of fellowship to men of every class who were earnest workers for the uplifting and Christianising of the masses. Sometime before he died I met with him at some special Church services in a large tent at Morecambe, when I saw that his young life was quickly tending to the grave. Shortly after that I walked with him one Sunday afternoon to the meeting at Calf Cop, Lower Bentham, which was the last time I met him. Such men as he and his brother were a credit and a spiritual force to any Christian Society.

Miss Leeming

Miss Leeming, Temperance Hotel and Boarding-house keeper. A few years ago the premises, once occupied as a chandlers shop and some cottages, came into the possession of Miss Leeming, when she built on a portion of the site nearer the street a substantial temperance hotel and boarding-house. When I went through it and saw what a substantial and commodious building it was, I could not but admire the pluck of the proprietress in undertaking such a responsibility. It is quite a credit to the village, and a useful adjunct to the temperance movement. I think Miss Leeming is a native of Bentham parish. Her father, Thomas Leeming, was a fresh old man when he was eighty years of age. I frequently used to meet him at this time of life at religious meetings at Brook House, Longber Road. He told me that when Bentham Mill was burnt down, May 19th, 1803, his mother carried him in her arms, he being a baby, to a crowd of farmers and their families on a knoll in Upper Greystone Gill, who were looking at the fire.

Further Tradesmen

Daniel Whitehead, potato dealer. Daniel is a descendant of the Whitehead family of Escewbeck, mentioned in an earlier article. One of the brothers who attended Collingwood School when I did afterwards removed to America, and as many of the family were long-lived, he may still be living. Daniel for many years lived at the Friends estate at Calf Cop, with an old uncle, and for some time after his uncles decease.

Christopher Oldfield, coal dealer, and John Oldfield, farmer and butter dealer. Though I have some recollection of their ancestors, not sufficiently to make any remarks. It is the same with Fred Shuttleworth, draper and grocer; Mr. Dodding, Punch Bowl Inn; and T. W. Sagar, schoolmaster. John Parker, late Miss Foster, grocer and draper. I remember the Parker family living near the Wenning, a little on the north side of the Punch Bowl Inn. I knew Miss Foster, but I was better acquainted with her father. Her uncle John I knew when I was a boy, and his son John. They were connected with the Parish Church, either as sextons or members of the Church choir. Also John Parker, who married into Edward Fosters family.

Joshua Maudsley, Sun Dial Inn. I remember his ancestors living on a farm at the north end of the village, where the late Rev. C. Thompson, already mentioned as a Collingwood scholar, was brought up. I still remember one or two of the boys attending the upper village Grammar School. I remember well Mrs. Maudsleys grandfather, old Richard Dean. He was the village fiddler, and in addition to his ordinary occupation, he used to teach a dancing school. I remember a Mrs. Dean, a widow of one of his sons, making me carry a message for her in 1830 to a friend of hers in the neighbourhood of London. Richard Deans musical talent was frequently in demand on festive occasions.

The firm of Messrs. Ford, Ayrton & Co., are mentioned in the 4th article. Some years before Mr. Ford came to the village, I was pretty well acquainted with the Fords of Morecambe Lodge, Yealand. The two brothers and Miss Ford took great interest in the "*Sketches of Village Life*", by "*Eavesdropper*", as they appeared for twenty weeks in succession in the columns of the **Lancaster Guardian**. The two brothers and their sister never refused to help me in any charitable work I was engaged in, therefore it is a pleasure to revive the recollection of their kind deeds. I may say, as far as I know Mr. Ford, he inherits the family generosity, and is always ready to give a helping hand where needed, outside his own Friends' Society, and outside his politics. He, like other political leaders and promoters of different schemes of education, sanitary reform, &c., comes in contact with leading men of opposite schemes, when things do not always move smoothly. A man who has a mind of his own, and the courage of his opinions, is sure to be snarled at by cowards, both in political and religious movements. When I came to Ingleton in 1854, many vile things as well as false were said of me because I dared to stand up for political and religious freedom. It may be boasting, but its true, I never met with a foe either present or in print whom I feared to face, and why? - because a good old book, much despised by multitudes of the present day, taught me in my youth, "*In deeds right and true, fear no man.*"

Mr. Ayrton, Mr. Fords partner, though a zealous friend of the Church of England, is generously fair with men who differ from him, and is one of those men who take a pleasure in giving "*God speed you*" in every good work for the human race. I was very pleased with the address he gave at Sedbergh, on needful church reform, and which appeared in the **Lancaster Guardian**. The leading topic of the address was that the services of laymen of piety and good common sense ought to be more extensively utilised for the benefit of the church. The Church of England is not the narrow system that many of its clergymen and members represent it to be. How few of them avail themselves of laymen to read the lessons in country churches, and when they do it is generally the squire or some gentlemen in position. There are many laymen in the Church of England who would be a great help to the clergy in missionary work, and visiting the sick if they were encouraged. It is to be hoped that Mr. Ayrton will persevere in his forward movement until some of the things which he recommended shall be brought into practice in his own parish.

As it is somewhat a delicate matter to mention names of persons in the way I have done in this article, I hope I have not transgressed, as I have the kindest feelings towards all the tradesmen of the village, and shall always be glad to hear that the community is prosperous and dwelling in peace. In my last weeks article I described Mr. Walker as keeper of the Colne Wesleyan Chapel. I find now that it is the Primitive Methodist Chapel.

No.11 (15th May, 1897)

The closing article of this series should be on the building improvements which have taken place in the tradesmens shops, working mens homes, &c., since 1820, but my present knowledge of later improvements is too inadequate for me to undertake. In place of such an article some recollection of the two Benthams may not be without interest. There were many things in the far past which bore resemblance in the two villages. The building and opening of a tower on Ingleborough was a memorable event in the history of the parish.

The Hospice Tower

This heading was the proposed heading of the new building indicating that the erection was to be a general benefit to all tourists and the public generally who might ascend the venerable mountain. It was a matter which interested all the neighbouring villages, hamlets, and even persons living in more distant towns. Mr. Hornby Roughsedge, of Bentham House, asked to be representative of the two Mills Company and the Lords of Ingleton Manor. As the two villages were equally interested in the movement it is only reasonable to include it in the reminiscences. Of late years I have only met with three old men who remembered the event, and were present at the opening. The late Mr. John Scott, and Mr. William Harrison, of Clapham, and Mr. J. Thomas Coates, who is now in his 84th year of his age. A year or two ago he told me that the event took place when he was in the 16th year of his age, which would be in 1830. He also told me that many gentlemen contributed to the building fund. It will be taken for granted that there was no easy matter to take material to the summit of the mountain.

There was one local advantage, there was plenty of stone within easy reach. The timber, lime, &c., were carted on a road branching from the old Ingleton and Clapham turnpike, near Newby Cote. The building of a tower on Ingleborough was viewed in different aspects through a wide district. While some persons looked upon it as a wild goose chase, which was sure to prove a failure, others thought that a tower on Ingleborough would not only be an attraction to mountain climbers but a convenience in which they might rest and take their portable refreshments. Though the lords of the manor might use the Tower as a shooting box, still it was well understood that it would always be accessible to the public. During the erection of the tower spying glasses and telescopes were used in clear weather in the surrounding villages to see what progress was being made in what was pronounced one of the wonders of Lunesdale. When the building was near its completion great preparations were made for its opening. The promoters of the Tower decided to make it a memorable event and a historical record.

The Opening of the Hospice Tower

The opening took place in the summer, and the day proved auspicious for the opening. People from every quarter of the compass were on their way from the two

Benthams, Ingleton, and the neighbouring villages. The centre of attraction was convenient for Ingleton and Clapham, consequently many persons availed themselves of the opportunity. There were also a number of gentlemen present to witness the proceedings. The chief features of the day were feasting, racing, drinking, and at night drunkenness, and mischievous rowdiness. The tower was a circular and substantial building with a dome roof. A round stone table for refreshments was fixed to the centre. The door and windows were made of strong material on account of the terrible winds which sweep over the summits plain from the north-west and the north-east. To human appearance it looked as if it would resist the winter storms for ages with occasional repairing. The memorable event took place with great rejoicing and much shouting. Mr. Roughsedge and many of his friends were there to take part in the opening ceremony. The racecourse was round the summit of the hill, which was about a mile. In one race twice round, Bark Smith, a well-known Ingleton coal miner, won the first prize, Kit Foster of Yarsber the second, and a Clapham man of the name of Parker the third. There were more races, but the one mentioned was the principal. Money was collected from the spectators to meet expenses.

Mr. Roughsedge, Mr. Overend, and their friends left for home some time before the drunken rows began and the work of mischief was completed. Thus drink and rowdyism inflicted ruin and desecration on an ornamental and useful building which had been put up at great expense and much labour for the benefit of mountain climbers as well as for the convenience of a shooting box in the grouse season. The great mischief done at the close of the memorable gala so grieved and annoyed Mr. Roughsedge and the friends who had planned and carried out the building of "*Hospice Tower*" that they would undertake no repairs, so that in the course of a few years it became a mass of ruins. When the door and windows were broken the torrent of winter rains and howling winds had free access to its interior and brought down its dome. The ruins lie in to a heap near the south-west of the mountains edge and within sight of all the villages and towns westward as far as Lancaster and Morecambe as a monument of the sad effects of intoxicating drinks.

Deeds of Mischief on Saturday Nights, etc.

Occasionally the frolics of the young men of Bentham were carried out on a large scale. The reason why this was done on Saturday nights was because the young men indulged more freely in drink than at other times, and usually sat at the public houses until midnight. This was at the time when publicans had the free sale of drink day and night from the beginning of the year to its close. The young men somewhat elated under the potent influence of John Barleycorn, began their midnight frolic as soon as they considered that the villagers had fallen asleep. Shop signs were pulled down, and with washing pots, dolly tubs, gates, doors, cartwheels, and every imaginable thing that could be carried away were laid on the front of the Brown Cow Inn and the two adjoining shops. There was one redeeming trait in those midnight rangers, they did not break any of the things which they had deposited on the pavement. It may easily be imagined what were the feelings of those persons who on the Sunday morning found that their pots, pans, &c., had been taken away. It was also fun for those young men to mix up with the lookers on while the owners of lost property picked out their articles from the confused medley. Such a jumble of domestic and other articles left an indelible impression on my mind so that after a space of seventy five years I can recall the sight as it then appeared.

Gun Powder Plot Mischief

The young men of both Upper and Lower Bentham delighted in the fun and mischief which attended the commemoration of the Gunpowder Plot. Some young men of that day were reckless as to what was taken of other mens combustibles. Some of the young men at Lairgill Row on such occasions were desperadoes. They were far from being particular as to the stealing of materials to keep up what they termed a good blaze. When the fire began to fail parties were sent out to the fields and the backyards of houses to procure anything that would burn - hedge stakes, old rails, gates, or any other procurable combustible that would keep up the blaze.

They were not particular as to the place on which they fixed for making the fire. I remember that it took place on one occasion on the highway between the two villages. It happened to be on a night when old Roger Carr's High Mill wagons had to pass there on the way to Lancaster. There was a stampede when the young men heard the rumble of the wagon wheels, which made them flee to the adjoining fields, where in the darkness they were out of sight and hearing. It may be imagined what was the terror of the drivers when they saw their way barred by a wall of fire. As they could not think of making a retreat, they began in good earnest to battle with the fire until it was sufficiently reduced for the passage of their horses, &c. Whilst this was going on the young men concealed in the darkness could see the efforts the carters made to scatter the fire brands. When the wagons had gone some distance they made their appearances and piled up their smoking faggots for a final blaze before their retreat homewards. Such deeds of daring mischief took place long before the time of the Peelers, and when many of the parish constables only laughed at such youthful frolics. Many of them knew that in their earlier days they had been guilty of similar practices. Some years before the police came into use in the two villages a moral reform took place among the young men, and such acts of mischief became things of the past.

Old Customs of Mirth Which Have Passed Away

Collop Monday and Pancake Tuesday were notable days in the calendar in my youth. On the Monday it was usual for boys and girls, and even poor women, to wander from door to door in the village and to the outside farmsteads, crying out, *"Please give me a collop."* This custom has entirely gone. Though pancake Tuesday is still kept up, some of its merry-making customs have disappeared. It was usual for parties to meet together to make a pancake feast. This generally took place in the evening, when the days work was done. A certain number of pancakes had to be eaten by each person, and the one that failed to eat his or her share was carried to the midden. When the man had to carry the woman, and the woman the man, the fun reached its highest pitch. At this date it was only considered a frolic of the season, and no one thought there was any indecency in the custom. Such things would be measured by the age in which they were done, and not by the advanced close of the nineteenth century. Those who have moved in a Continental carnival at Shrovetide will not think there was any ill in a pancake feast of the olden time and its consequences.

Lifting Days at Eastertide

This custom which was common in the two villages at the beginning of the present century, and for many years subsequently, is now one of the things of the past. On Easter Monday the men lifted the women, and on the Tuesday the women lifted the men. To lift the women two men joined their hands right and left, after which the women sat between their arms and were heaved or lifted up generally three times. In my boyhood I used to see the men take them by the shoulders and feet and throw them up with a once, twice and three times. I can say that in carrying out this custom with the women the men strictly avoided what might have been considered rudeness. It is written in a document in the Tower of London that some ladies and maids of honour took King Edward the First in his bed and lifting him after the custom of the times, for which the King paid no less a sum than what would be equal at the present day to £400. It is recorded that a certain clergyman was staying at a certain inn for an hour or two on Easter Tuesday when four lusty women rushed into the room saying, "*We have to lift you.*" "*To lift me*", he said, "*What do you mean?*" "*Why, your reverence, weve come to lift you cause its Easter Tuesday.*" "*Lift me because its Easter Tuesday? I dont understand. Is there any such custom here?*" "*Yes, to be sure, why, dont you know? All us women was lifted yesterday, and us women lifts the men today in turn. And in coorse its our reights and duties to lift em.*" As his reverence had no wish to be lifted he compromised the matter by a gift of half-a-crown.

The pace egging ceremony which used to excite a good deal of merriment at Easter, especially amongst the children, is amongst the things of the past. Also drinking mulled ale on Easter Sunday evening. Even some of the villagers who made more than an ordinary show of religion did not think it unbecoming to take a glass of mulled ale and a pipe of tobacco at one of the village inns on an Easter Sunday evening. It is well that many of our old English customs have passed away.

The headstone on the grave of Joseph Carr, in Ingleton cemetery.

Death of Mr. Jos. Carr, of Ingleton

(18th February, 1899)

It is with unfeigned regret we have this week to announce the death of Mr. Joseph Carr, which occurred at his residence, Hollin Tree, Ingleton, on Thursday morning. Mr. Carr was a native of Bentham, and had lived practically all his life in the district, working in his early days as a silk dresser at Wray, Bentham, and other places, but for more than half a century he has been closely identified with the village of Ingleton, of the scenic beauties of which he was the earliest explorer and advocate.

Probably the deceased gentleman was best known as the district correspondent of the **Lancaster Guardian**, in which capacity he has acted for the long period of forty years. Latterly his work in this capacity has been confined to the village of Ingleton alone, but at one time his district covered not merely Ingleton, but Kirkby Lonsdale, Burton-in-Lonsdale, Bentham, and all the intervening hamlets and townships. In this vocation he was brought in contact with men of all classes and creeds, both in religion and politics, and his unflinching integrity, straightforwardness, determined adherence to what he believed to be right, and at the same time his amiability and thorough human kindness made him respected, esteemed, and honoured by everyone. Though practically self-taught he had a facile pen, was a ready and graceful writer on a variety of subjects, and rarely a week elapsed without the publication of letters and special articles which he had found time to indite in the midst of his ordinary avocations. He was a particularly expert writer of *"dialect"*. More than half a century ago he contributed to the **Guardian** a series of articles entitled *"Sketches of Village Life"* by *"Eavesdropper"*, which were exceedingly interesting and widely read, and which when published afterwards in book form commanded a ready sale.

Chiefly, however, Mr. Carr will be remembered, as he deserves to be, for his long and persistent advocacy of the claims of Ingleton to be considered a health resort. Practically he was the first explorer and discoverer of the wild and romantic scenery with which the district abounds; he published the first guide to Ingleton, and was the pioneer of the first Improvement Company, of which he acted as Secretary until it gave way to the modern companies. It is divulging no secret to say that Mr. Carr's self-sacrificing devotion to the work of developing the district brought him more hard knocks than anything else, especially from some quarters, but there is little doubt that but for his persistent advocacy and force of character Ingleton would even now have been comparatively unknown. He laboured, and others are reaping the fruits of his labours. Mr. Carr has been identified with Nonconformity all his life, and for a long series of years he was an acceptable local preacher - first in connection with the Wesleyans, and later with the Free Methodists - filling appointments not only in the villages, but at Lancaster, Southport, Preston, Kendal, and other places. But in religious views, as in other matters, he was a singularly broad-minded man, and was always ready, so far as he possibly could, to help forward every good cause, irrespective of creed or party.

Details of the last illness of the deceased gentleman, who had passed his eightieth year, have not yet been forwarded, and a fuller account of his career is deferred until next week. We understand that the remains of the deceased gentleman will be interred at Ingleton on Monday next, the cortege being formed to leave Hollin Tree at 2.30 p.m.

The Late Mr. J. Carr, of Ingleton

(25th February, 1899)

The death of Mr. Joseph Carr, of Ingleton, which occurred, as intimated in our last issue, at an early hour on Thursday 16th inst., has evoked expressions of regret through a very wide district. The deceased gentleman, who was in his 87th year, was a native of Bentham, and was educated at the Grammar School there, under the late Rev. J. Marshall. Subsequently he was apprenticed to the woollen business, and later went to France to perfect his knowledge in this direction. There he came in for somewhat severe handling from the woollen workers, who had a notion that he was a manufacturer's son sent over to learn the secrets of the trade. He returned to England after about 18 months' stay, but afterwards went out to Boulogne as a missionary and had charge of a small church there. Mr. Carr was in France during stirring times, for he was an eye-witness of the unsuccessful descent upon Boulogne by the late Louis Napoleon, and saw the fight in the water at which Napoleon was taken prisoner. He was also compelled by the gendarmes to assist in digging graves in the sand for the burial of those who were slain in the encounter. A few days later he was in the market-place in Boulogne when the white-haired Louis Phillipe came to thank the inhabitants for having captured his enemy, and told his landlady of the reception given to the Monarch. Her comment was prophetic, for she said, "*Oh, it is Louis Phillipe today, Napoleon tomorrow!*" In a year or two the positions of the two were completely reversed, and Louis Phillipe was a fugitive in England. On Mr. Carr's return to England he was appointed pastor of the Independent Church, Kirkby Lonsdale. A few years later he married Miss Balderston, of Hollin Tree, Ingleton, where, about 1854, he took up his residence, and where he remained until his death.

An account of his literary and social work at Ingleton, and also of his indefatigable efforts on behalf of the Free Churches in various parts of the district appeared in our last issue, and it only remains to add that of late years Mr. Carr had suffered considerably from chest complaints, and a severe attack of bronchitis terminated fatally after a few days illness. The only survivor of his family is a daughter who has resided with him at Hollin Tree and who desires to express her thanks and gratitude to the numerous friends who have tendered sympathy and help during the time of her great bereavement.

In the course of his sermon at St. Mary's, Ingleton, on Sunday morning last, the Vicar (Rev. J. Turner) made touching reference to the loss sustained by Mr. Carr's death. He said: "*The death of Mr. Carr removes a landmark from this parish, whether we look at his great age, or at his many and varied activities in regard to the affairs of this community. He was not connected with us for the greater part of his life in the Church, but* his later years manifested a much greater degree of friendliness than was, I believe, the case before, and it was, I know, his wish to die in communion with the Church. `The Church of England', I have often heard him say, `is a great power for good in the land', and that, I believe, is the opinion of many Nonconformists, though for various reasons they may prefer to walk in their own ways. I can personally bear witness to many acts of friendliness from Mr. Carr, and honestly say that I much regret his loss. In regard to the general good of this place I think there can be but one opinion, that it was his desire to promote its good. It is well known how unceasing were his efforts in endeavouring to make known the natural beauties of this district, and on that account he has been fittingly described as one of, if not the `maker of Ingleton'. Moreover, it was certainly his wish to promote the moral welfare of the people; in temperance and wholesome living he was certainly a preacher of righteousness. Not more than a fortnight before his death, speaking about the Bible, he wrote to me, `If it had not been for its wise and pithy sayings on health and how to preserve and prolong it, I should never have attained my present age of 86 years. I have in remembrance many young men 60 years ago who constitutionally had a fairer prospect of reaching a good old age than I, and yet through intemperance and other excesses have been dead long ago.' He bore unceasing witness to the value of temperance and to the evils of intemperance and I do not think that though we may at times many of us have differed with him, yet that we can doubt that his intentions were good, and that in his motives he had at heart the welfare of his fellows, even if there may have seemed some self-will and want of proper judgement in his actions at times. He has lived to an age far beyond the allotted years of man, and will, I think, be much missed and regretted. He has now gone from this life to another, and there let us hope he will find mercy and acceptance with Him whom he wished to serve in this life, who is the rewarder of those who diligently seek Him."

The funeral, which took place at the Ingleton Cemetery on Monday, was of a public character, many of the inhabitants of Ingleton attending to show their respect for the character of the deceased gentleman, whilst representatives of the Nonconformist churches at Settle, Clapham, Bentham, and other places were also present. Amongst those present were: Mr. L. M. Sibbald (Glasgow), Mr. and Mrs. R. B. Cragg (Skipton), Mr. and Mrs. Ellershaw (Ingleton), Mr. W. Rhodes, J.P., Mr. Leach, Mr. Brookes, Mr. R. Sanderson, Mr. W. Knowles (Bentham), Mr. W. H. Watson representing the Lancaster Guardian, etc. The coffin, which was of polished oak with brass handles, was supplied by Messrs. Whalley and Sons, and was carried by eight bearers - tenants and neighbours; it was covered with beautiful wreaths from many relatives and friends. A short service was held at St. Mary's Church, where a large congregation assembled, and where the first part of the service for the burial of the dead was conducted by the Vicar (Rev. J. Turner), assisted by Rev. J. Harrison, Vicar of Barbon. The hymns "*Soldiers of Christ*" and "*Rock of ages*" were sung, and the service was a very impressive one throughout. The remainder of the service, at the cemetery, was read by the Rev. J. Turner. Along the route from Hollin Tree to the Cemetery the blinds of the shops and houses were drawn, and the funeral took place amid every demonstration of sympathy and respect.

List of Subscribers

Mrs. M. J. Adams, Beckenham
John & Yvonne Allen, Bentham Lodge
W. S. Armstrong, Giggleswick
Bernard Armstrong, Thickrash Brow
Ralph & Pat Atkinson, Robin Lane

Arthur Bainbridge, Barton, Preston
Colin Roy Baines, Main Street
Jacqueline D. Baines, Main Street
Lisa Marie Baines, Main Street
Colin & Heather Baines, Main Street
Lucy Ball, Caton
Melanie Banks, Robin Lane
Lorna Barnes, Higher Westhouse
Kenneth Barnes, Keighley
Miss D. Batty, Leeds
G. J. Bentham, Bromham, Beds.
David & Wendy Bentham, Urmston
John Bentham, Turn, Ramsbottom
Margaret Lockwood Bolster, Burnaby, B.C., Canada
Steve Brett, Burnley
George M. Brett, Accrington
Richard A. Brooke, Cheadle Hulme
Colin & Shirley Brown, Springfield
Irene & Geoff Brown, Westhouse
F. M. Butterfield, Butts Lane

Erica Cameron, Burton-in-Lonsdale
Mrs. Isabel Carr, Lowther Hill Farm
Barrie & Kathy Cartledge, Oysterber Farm
Neville & Diane Chant, Bank Top Cottages
Joe Cherry, Huyton, Liverpool (2 copies)
Gordon Christie, Barrow in Furness (2 copies)
Colin Clapham, Lanefoot
Mr. & Mrs. D. Clapham, Mewith Lane
Rhoda Coates, Main Street

J. Dalton, Scotforth
Dr. John M. Dawson, Bromley (2 copies)
Mike Derbyshire, Quernmore
Poppy Dowell, Portpatrick

Colin William Easterby, Sutton in Craven
Doth & Ian Edmondson-Noble, Victoria Buildings
R. Ellershaw, Goodenber Road
Alexander William Ellershaw, Banks Way
Leslie Ely, Lakeber Drive

Mrs. Dorothy Faraday, Robin Lane
Julie (nee Foster) & Clifford Fisher, Low Bentham Road
Brian Fletcher, Barley, Burnley
Christopher J. N. Fletcher, Cheltenham
Norman Foster, Ulverston
Mrs. J. A. Foster, Lytham St. Annes, ex Barton House
William Ronald Frankland, Goodenber Road
Mrs. J. Freeman, Ware
Mark Frost, Victoria Buildings

Mr. & Mrs. Galvin, Lane Head
Emmeline Garnett, Wray
Mike & Jean Gathergood, Robin Lane
B. Green-Hughes, Robin Lane
R. G. K. Gudgeon, Lawkland
Tom Guy, Fern Cottage

Mrs. Edith Hamilton, Kirkby Lonsdale
Howard Hammersley, Preston (2 copies)
Michael Hart, Mewith
A. C. Hart, Darlington
Kim S. Hicks, nee Marshall, Oakham
Thelma Holland, Millhouses
Dr. Christopher S. Holmes, Whalley
R. E. Huddleston, Low Oak Head
Michael E. Hutchinson, Otley
Elizabeth Hutchinson, Settle
Keith Hutchinson, Keighley
Reg Hutchinson, Robin Lane

Mary Ireland, Low Bentham Road

Ann Jefferies, nee Fisher, Low Bentham Road
Dr. Rosemary Jenkins, Clapham
William J. Joel, Station Road
Mrs. Kathleen Johnston, Cowan Bridge
Peter Joslin, Morecambe

Bill Kennedy, Lakeber Ave.
Henry & Stephany Ann Kirkwood, nee Reid, Wennington
Doug & Joyce Knapp, Summer Hill
Mrs. E. Knapp, Overton, Wakefield

Hazel Lawson, nee Wilcock, Lakeber Drive
Edwin Leeming, Robin Lane
Stella Longland, West Stonegate
Betty Longmate, Bolton

John Lynch, Oswaldtwistle
Garnett Makinson, Halton
Shirley Marsden-McHale, Summer Hill
Anthony A. Marshall, Kendal
Peter E. Marshall, Cricklade
Thomas Bateman Marshall, Bentham Hall
Sara Mason, Tatham Fells
Donald Mellor, Keighley
E. Metcalfe, Barrow
Julie Middleton, Lakeber Ave.
Joy & Teddy Morgan, Links Drive

David Nortcliffe, Pye Busk Close
North Yorkshire Library, Northallerton (4 copies)

Old Yorkshire Magazine, Otley

John & Eileen Perkins, Durham
Anthony Petyt, Wakefield

Ann Rathbone, Warrington
Mrs. Irene Redhead, Ingleton
Mrs. Mary Redhead, Ingleton
Mr. & Mrs. C. Reid, Mewith
Michael Robert Reid, Woking
Mrs. Anne Rhodes, Hull
Anne Riley, Stourbridge
T. Ian Roberts, Settle
Neil H. Roberts, Giggleswick
Jo & Mick Ryan, Sevenoaks (2 copies)

Brenda Saul, nee McClelland, Mytton
Mrs. Shirley Saville, Hull
Adrian & Margie Simper, Station Road
Mildred Benson Slater, nee Lamb, Furness Drive
Fred Smickersgill, Morecambe
John Morgan Smith, Duke Street
Mary Smith, Waterfoot
Tony Smith, Gillingham
G. Smith, Settle
Mrs. F. A. Smith, Greenhills
Mavis & Geoffrey Sutcliffe, Low Bentham Road

Andrea & Steve Taylor, Springfield Terrace
Mary Taylor, Tatham Fells
Janice Tolson, Clitheroe
Kathleen Tomlinson, Colne
Geoffrey Townson, Totnes
Katherine Townson, Settle

Peter Garnett Holmes Townson, Alton
Tom Townson, Romford
Kin Walker, Gerrards Cross
J. S. Warbrick, Robin Lane
James & Jean West, Lairgill
Frank Wheildon, Valley Field
Dr. T. M. Whitaker, Greenfoot Barn
Nigel Wilcock, Robin Lane
J. B. & M. M. Wildman, Mount Pleasant
C. M. Wildman, Kirkby Malham
Fraser W. T. Wilkins, P.O., Main Street
Bernard Williams, Robin Lane
Margaret Wilmhurst, Garstang
John Wilson, Tatham
Simone Wilson, Brownedge
Joyce Wolfendale, Eccles
Duncan Worsick, Bentham Old Hall
Ken Wray, Caton

Index of Surnames

Alderson 46, 56, 96
Alexander 36
Altham 82, 90, 114
Arkwright 43
Armistead 33, 44, 111, 117, 122
Atkinson 20, 47, 55, 72, 76
Auton 55
Ayrton 23, 77, 129

Bailey 18, 21, 126
Bailiff 33
Balderston 76, 117
Band 55
Banks 74, 122, 124
Barker 33, 39, 76
Barnes 119
Barrow 112
Bateson 82, 92, 119
Battersby 11, 21, 31, 33
Bean 124
Bell 36
Bellman 26, 39, 64, 113
Benison 41
Benn 68, 74, 122
Benson 108
Bentham 33, 41, 43, 52, 55, 127
Berry 77
Bibby 53, 55, 58
Bickerstaff 14, 39
Blackburn 17, 19, 52, 59
Blezard 83
Bond 64, 70, 86
Bottomley 55,
Bowker 18, 55, 64
Boyd 126
Bradley 54,
Bradshaw 33
Braithwaite 26, 71, 125
Brayshaw 109
Brook 49, 107,
Brown 40, 41, 46
Bunting 102
Burns 118
Burrow 20, 30, 33, 55, 58, 83, 110
Burrows 21, 48
Burton 11, 18, 33, 60

Bush 50, 55
Butler 45, 81, 104, 107
Butterfield 21, 31, 47

Cadman 119
Camm 13, 59, 89, 119
Cantsfield 102
Carr 14, 17, 19, 33, 46, 50, 56, 59, 63, 132
Carter 83, 93
Caverley 55
Charnley 17, 24, 54, 71
Chester 111
Child 71
Clapham 41, 48, 55, 83
Clark 33, 41, 122
Clarke 30, 45
Clayton 104
Cliborn 60
Coates 48, 52, 56, 73, 96, 109, 130
Cocking 22, 83
Collingwood 52, 108, 125
Constantine 59, 122
Cook 33
Cooper 56
Coulam 51, 73, 74
Cousins 38
Cowgill 104
Crawford 72
Croft 33, 108
Cumberland 24, 56, 83, 92, 114, 118, 125

Darnley 116, 120
Davidson 45
Davies 122, 124
Davis 74, 115
Dawson 73
Dean 128
Dennis 14
Dewsbury 104, 111
Dodding 128
Dodgson 97, 127
Dowbiggin 83
Downham 108
Dyer 119
Dymond 115

Earnshaw 98
Easterby 31, 48, 61
Edwards 118
Ellershaw 11, 23, 33, 41, 45, 60, 82, 107, 109
Ellethorne 77
Elletson 37, 94, 118
Ellis 104
Evans 57
Exton 69

Faraday 15, 46
Farneworth 104, 111
Farrer 83
Featherstone 104
Fell 104
Field 104
Fielding 104
Fishe 104
Fletcher 55
Ford 98, 117, 119, 129
Foster 48, 55, 83, 84, 107, 128, 131
Foxcroft 78

Garlick 52, 55
Garnett 107
Geldard 18, 30, 72
Gerrard 102
Gillow 31
Goodhall 104, 125
Gornall 19
Gorrill 52, 55, 127
Grayson 58, 60
Green 76, 82
Greenep 19, 30, 32, 39, 47, 55
Griffiths 55
Guy 11, 18, 21, 33, 42, 46, 52

Hall 104, 111, 117, 124
Hardy 30
Harger 72
Harker 55
Harris 118
Harrison 55, 60, 130
Hartley 40
Hay 20
Head 30
Heaton 11, 32, 33, 41, 42, 46, 71, 90
Hemmingway 55
Hewitson 22

Hewitt 55
Hind 47, 55
Hindson 86
Hird 73
Hodgson 37
Hodkinson 126
Hogg 43, 52, 55
Hoggarth 65
Holbeck 47, 55
Holden 107, 108
Holdsworth 55
Holmes 17, 21, 30, 33, 39, 47, 55, 58, 60, 62, 83, 125, 127
Hopkins 104
Hornby 33, 41, 56, 59, 83, 113, 121
Howard 74
Howson 46, 73, 98
Huggon 22, 33
Hully 31
Hutchinson 55, 86

Ibbotson 122
Irvine 55

Jackman 21, 46, 51, 55
Jackson 18, 50, 52, 55, 72, 93, 95, 119, 127
James 86
Jenkins 73
Johnson 11, 20, 25, 29, 32, 36, 43, 83, 86, 92, 100
Jones 121
Joy 107, 110
Just 110

Kaye 114
Kendal 11, 18, 82, 114, 118
Kent 122
Kidd 55
King 14, 78
Knowles 20, 35, 43, 46, 54, 72, 114, 121, 127

Lamb 51, 55
Lambert 14
Langham 74, 121
Langstreth 21, 47, 63
Leach 51
Leak 15, 18, 30, 33, 42, 127

Leeming 48, 72, 92, 118, 128
Leson 104
Llewellyn 55
Lord 92
Lord Milton 63
Lord Morphet 63
Lowth 53
Lowther 22, 53, 104
Lupton 33, 71, 104,

Marquand 73
Marsden 42, 127
Marshall 31, 45, 51, 55, 81, 125
Marton 104
Maudsley 36, 52, 55, 64, 128
McClellan 118
McMahon 117, 122
Melling 11, 15, 30, 33, 42, 44, 53
Metcalfe 33, 55, 90
Middlebrook 18, 19, 33, 43, 46, 51
Minikin 77
Mirescue 104
Moore 33
Morphet 51, 55, 83
Mountain 92
Muncaster 30

Newhouse 75
Nicholson 30, 46, 62

Oldfield 128
Otterburn 104
Overend 11, 25, 30, 61, 63, 65, 71, 78, 107, 109, 131

Parker 11, 18, 22, 25, 30, 35, 37, 64, 75, 82, 94, 104, 113, 119, 128, 131
Parkin 33
Parrington 55
Pattinson 40, 122
Peel 41
Perkin 60
Phillipson 30, 48, 55, 73, 97, 117, 122
Phipps 14, 59, 75
Pope 114
Preston 107
Pritt 14
Procter 31, 43, 47, 51, 55, 59, 84
Pullen 115

Quinlan 19, 46, 51

Raby 22
Ray 108
Redmayne 61, 83
Rhodes 55
Rice 20, 21, 47, 51, 72, 114, 122
Robertshaw 55
Robinson 46, 55, 63, 105, 107, 116
Roughsedge 11, 25, 31, 34, 37, 43, 63, 74, 77, 100, 130,

Sagar 128
Sanderson 30, 47, 55, 58, 73, 119
Saul 73, 119
Savage 71
Scott 109, 130
Sedgwick 13, 31, 33, 41, 51, 53, 59
Seed 42, 51, 55, 58, 69, 72, 127
Seeds 42
Sellars 83
Shackleton 26
Sharp 21, 33
Shaw 109
Shepherd 33, 40, 54, 55
Sherlock 102, 104,
Shuttleworth 30, 74, 122, 128
Silverwood 33
Sinclair 95
Skirrow 14, 29, 30, 33, 46, 81, 90, 105
Slinger 21, 30, 33, 44, 46, 53, 55
Smith 30, 48, 50, 55, 73, 83, 124, 131
Smithers 23, 33
Snayden 104, 111
Snell 72
Speight 109
Stackhouse 13
Stephenson 19, 30, 33, 40, 46, 55, 126
Stewart 43
Stokes 117, 122
Stordy 114
Swainson 11, 30, 108, 110
Swales 33
Swetynge 104
Swinbank 18, 33
Swithenbank 55

Tatham 55, 83
Taylor 91

Teale 100, 110
Tempest 65, 95
Tennant 11, 14, 30, 90
Thies 117, 119
Thompson 48, 55, 72, 92, 128
Thornborrow 82, 83, 91
Thornton 30, 43, 48, 63, 83, 85, 88, 90
Titterington 24, 33, 45, 48, 58, 81, 83
Titterton 31
Toulman 92
Toulmin 18
Townley 55
Townsend 58
Townson 26, 33, 39, 42, 64, 83, 90, 92, 107, 113, 117
Tunstall 11, 24, 33
Turner 55, 74
Twistleton 71

Umpleby 117
Uxor 107

Varley 14
Vickers 73
Vipond 15, 52

Walker 44, 74, 117, 122, 129
Wallace 82
Ward 19, 51, 83,
Wardroper 93
Wesley 98
Whitaker 118
Whitehead 88, 92, 128
Whittaker 45
Wigglesworth 23, 77
Wilcock 19, 30, 42, 48, 55, 58, 62, 83, 88, 113
Wildman 11, 33, 38, 43, 46, 48, 49, 55, 77, 91, 98
Wilkinson 33, 43, 107
Willan 19, 30, 33, 53, 55
Willans 18
Wilman 59
Wilson 30, 41, 44, 52, 55, 63, 86, 113
Winder 56
Wood 104
Wrathall 83
Wray 48, 107
Wright 117

Yeardly 113